D1114973

"Then **Levy** Said to **Kelly...**"

The Best Buffalo Bills Stories Ever Told

Jim Gehman

TRIUMPH
B O O K S

Copyright © 2008 by Jim Gehman

No part of this publication may be reproduced, stored in a retrieval system, or transmitted, in any form by any means, electronic, mechanical, photocopying, or otherwise, without the prior written permission of the publisher, Triumph Books, 542 S. Dearborn St., Suite 750, Chicago, Illinois 60605.

Triumph Books and colophon are registered trademarks of Random House, Inc.

Library of Congress Cataloging-in-Publication Data

Gehman, Jim, 1960–
Then Levy said to Kelly— : the best Buffalo Bills stories ever told / Jim Gehman.
    p. cm.
  Includes bibliographical references.
  ISBN-13: 978-1-60078-055-4
  ISBN-10: 1-60078-055-5
1. Buffalo Bills (Football team)—History. 2. I. Title II. Title: Best Buffalo Bills stories ever told.
  GV956.B83G44 2008
  796.333'640974797—dc22

                                    2008012332

This book is available in quantity at special discounts for your group or organization. For further information, contact:

Triumph Books
542 South Dearborn Street
Suite 750
Chicago, Illinois 60605
(312) 939-3330
Fax (312) 663-3557

Printed in U.S.A.
ISBN: 978-1-60078-055-4
Design by Patricia Frey

Photo Credits:
All photos courtesy of Getty Images unless otherwise indicated.

For my mom, Doris Gehman, and the rest of my family and friends. I realize how much my life has changed—the limitations—since the car accident, and I'm sorry.

And for Ralph C. Wilson Jr. and the men who have coached and played for his team, the Buffalo Bills. And for the fans that have supported the Bills throughout the years and called the team their own.

table of
contents

foreword

While growing up in Los Angeles, California, in the '40s and '50s, I dreamt of someday playing professional football as a quarterback in the NFL. And later, with that same dream, my coach at Occidental College told me if I worked hard—if I practiced more, lifted weights, and if I studied—I was the one player at Oxy who could make it in the NFL.

Drafted in 1957 by the Detroit Lions and traded to the Pittsburgh Steelers, I played in four games that season with the Steelers, and a year later I found myself on the taxi squad as the third-string quarterback of the New York Giants. And then after a brief sojourn in the Canadian Football League, I returned home to Southern California to play with the Chargers in the newborn American Football League. Two seasons, two games, and a severely broken finger later, I was on injured reserve and ended up as a Buffalo Bill in 1962.

I wanted to stay with the Chargers, no doubt about that. But when I realized that "doors don't close, that other doors don't open," as my mother used to say, Buffalo was going to be the right place for me. The very first game I played for the Bills in 1962 was against the Oakland Raiders, and I had a big brace on my finger, and I literally couldn't brush my teeth it hurt so bad. But the pain was tolerable because even though I had worn other uniforms in two different leagues, becoming a Buffalo Bill presented the opportunity to not only live out my childhood dream, but to be a part of two AFL championships as well.

The Bills then and now are a reflection of Ralph C. Wilson Jr. Wilson was one of the finest owners in the history of professional football and as responsible as any owner for the success of the American Football League and the National Football League. No one deserves to be in the Pro Football Hall of Fame more, and it's long overdue.

The Bills then and now are also a reflection of the tremendously devoted and loyal fans of Buffalo, New York. I truly believe
that football is America's greatest sport, and as football is uniquely
American, I believe that the Bills are uniquely Buffalo.

—Jack Kemp

foreword

My first experience with the Bills occurred when they chose me during the 1973 NFL draft. I actually had no idea where Buffalo was other than it was in New York state. And so the first thing I did was pull out a map.

As it turned out, I could not have found my way up there at a better time. The team was moving into a new stadium, the whole community seemed to be excited, and there was one teammate who was on the threshold of making history.

When O.J. Simpson broke the league's rushing record with 2,003 yards, he took us all along for the ride: the fans, the "Electric Company," and, well, me—a slightly nervous rookie quarterback from Louisiana. But over the next several years, I became less nervous and grew more confident.

There were a few games when the weather was really bad, we weren't winning, and we didn't have a good crowd, but you could tell that the Bills fans were true at heart. All they were looking for was a good effort and honest play. And if you played hard and you gave the effort, they could see it, and they appreciated it. And that's what I always liked about it; the fans always appreciated what we did.

It's amazing to me that I can still come back to Buffalo and be recognized and get the reception that I do from the fans. Yeah, I was cheered during my 12 seasons with the Bills, and I was certainly booed, as well. But through it all, I developed a real fondness for the city and its people, and I would like to think I became one of them.

I read with intent the development of the team—starting with Ralph Wilson, the only owner of the Buffalo Bills—and the fascinating stories of many players and coaches, some of whom were my teammates. Jim Gehman was able to communicate accurately their true life experiences in an easy-to-read style that gives one a greater insight and respect for the game.

Thank you, Jim, for taking the time and effort to write about Buffalo pride. And thank you, the reader, for your passion for the Bills and your support over all these years.

—Joe Ferguson

acknowledgments

I would like to thank Rick Azar, Sal Maiorana, and Jim Peters for sharing their experiences and providing guidance.

I also wish to thank Scott Berchtold, Joe Ferguson, Sandy Ferguson, Ardell Gehman, Joni Graham, Jack Kemp, Denny Lynch, Bona Park, Gregg Pastore, Cindy Seames, and whoever invented the computer's spell check for their assistance and contributions.

And finally, thanks to Tom Bast, Laine Morreau, and the staff of Triumph Books for not only the opportunity, but the patience and leadership they have shown throughout this project.

introduction

Buffalo's first victory in the American Football League occurred a year before its first game.

After he reportedly read a *New York Times* article about the upstart league in 1959, Ralph C. Wilson Jr., a highly successful insurance and trucking businessman from Detroit and a onetime minority owner of that city's National Football League Lions, contacted the AFL's principal organizer, Lamar Hunt, the son of a Dallas oil mogul, and spoke of his interest in the prospective Miami franchise. Wilson had a winter home near the Florida city and enjoyed the area. The local politicians did not share the snowbird's enthusiasm about the potential new league and denied his overtures about sharing the Orange Bowl with the University of Miami to use as a home field.

Hunt convinced the discouraged Wilson to stay involved in the venture and offered him what would be the eighth charter team in the league and the choice of locating the franchise in Buffalo, Louisville, Cincinnati, St. Louis, or Atlanta. Wilson had never traveled across the Canadian province of Ontario that separated his Michigan home from New York state's second-largest city. But after visiting Buffalo and, more specifically, War Memorial Stadium and listening to an impassioned pledge of support from *Buffalo Evening News* sports editor Paul Neville, Wilson doled out the $25,000 franchise fee, and the Bills were born.

Through the first four decades of the team's existence, Wilson witnessed heart-pounding championships, crushing defeats, a merge with the NFL, a move to a new stadium in suburban Orchard Park, and incredible support from people like himself, who loved the game of football.

During those first 40 years, the Bills were guided by 98 head and assistant coaches and had 808 men take the field with buffalo decals adorning the sides of their helmets. Some are enshrined in the Pro Football Hall of Fame. Some will be. Some should be. And some will have to pay the admission in order to step foot in the hallowed hall. They all, however, have one thing in common. They were Buffalo Bills.

chapter 1

The Birth of the Bills

The original home of the Bills, War Memorial Stadium housed two of Buffalo's first stars, Elbert Dubenion and Wray Carlton.
(Photo courtesy of WireImages)

A Golden Start

If nothing else, the Buffalo Bills opened the first season of the American Football League in 1960 with some outstanding speed on their roster. Namely, Elbert "Golden Wheels" Dubenion.

"I don't know how fast I was, but I was faster than anybody there," laughed the free-agent wide receiver from Bluffton College. "[Running back] Willmer Fowler was a Big Ten sprint champion, and I used to beat him. I didn't know who he was, actually. I didn't keep up with the Big Ten. I was fast enough not to get beat."

While Dubenion's quickness was clearly not questioned when Buffalo took the field at New York's Polo Grounds for its inaugural game against the Titans on September 11, his aim, well, that was a different story. "Tommy O'Connell was the quarterback, and I was supposed to get a reverse. But on the handoff, I didn't get close enough to get the ball because the left defensive end broke through, and if I had stayed close to the quarterback, I'd have got killed. I thought it was better O'Connell than me, so I got a little wider," Dubenion said with a chuckle. "That would have been the end of my career, because no one blocked him. O'Connell didn't see him coming. He had his back to him, so he was all right. But I saw him coming! Plus I had three fumbles. I almost got cut after that game. On the plane [after being beat 27–3, head coach] Buster Ramsey told me he was going to send me back home because I dropped several passes, too. I went back to Buffalo and packed my bags, but he didn't call me. So I went to practice. It was a day-to-day thing there for the following week."

Still a member of the team when the next game rolled around, the home opener against Denver, Dubenion made the coach happy that he had not placed the call. With one second remaining in the first half, Dubenion hauled in a 53-yard touchdown pass from O'Connell to put the Bills ahead, 13–6. He added a 56-yard touchdown reception late in the third quarter and finished the game, a 27–21 loss, with three catches for 112 yards and a sense that his job was a bit more secure.

"Buster said I was all right then. He wasn't going to send me back home. I felt that I had earned another week. Back then, when the NFL cut a guy, the AFL snatched him up," said Dubenion. "So you were watching the transactions to see if anybody in your position got cut. If you come in the locker room and see a guy about your size, uh-oh, hard practice today because he may be in my position. It was a little nerve-racking."

First Trip to the End Zone

Selected by Philadelphia of the NFL in 1959, Duke running back Wray Carlton did not fare too well during his contract talks, and he opted instead to play for Toronto of the Canadian Football League. But after just four games with the Argonauts, a proposed trade to Vancouver sat with him about as well as the failed negotiations with the Eagles. He packed up and returned home to North Carolina. Discouraged by the politics of the two leagues, Carlton began working for a local bank. His opinion about a pro football career would change, however, by simply answering the telephone.

"Lou Saban, who was with the Boston Patriots, called me. They had just formed a new league, and he came down a couple times and convinced me that I wanted to play," Carlton said. "I kind of wanted to come back and play some more. I was still young and virile and ready to go. I didn't really want to give it up, so he didn't have to convince me too much. When the AFL was formed, that gave a whole new league to a lot of people like me. I didn't really want to go to Philly, and they weren't going to trade my rights to anybody, so I was kind of stuck. I was very thankful that the league was formed because I really wanted to keep playing. I didn't want to quit, not at 22 years old. So I signed with Boston, went through [the 1960] training camp with them, and was traded to the Buffalo Bills. I got here maybe a week before the season started."

Buffalo began the AFL's inaugural season on September 11, 1960, with a game in New York's Polo Grounds, a 27–3 loss to the Titans. Carlton had seven carries for 13 yards. A week later in the home opener against Denver at War Memorial Stadium, he scored the Bills' first touchdown 4:53 into the second quarter on a one-yard run.

"I was listening to the radio a couple years ago, to a Buffalo station, and a trivia question popped up. The guy said, 'Who scored the Bills' first touchdown?' Everybody was saying, 'I don't know. I don't know.' And I'm thinking, 'I don't know who it was,'" laughed Carlton. "Then some guy called in and said, 'Wray Carlton.' I said, 'Whoa! That's amazing! I didn't even know that.' I never really thought about it. It never occurred to me that I was the one that scored the first touchdown."

Unfortunately for the Bills, Broncos cornerback Johnny Pyeatt scored the game's final touchdown on a 40-yard interception return in the fourth quarter. Denver won, 27–21.

chapter 2

Welcome to Buffalo, Kid!

Although George "Butch" Byrd was new to the Bills, his outstanding performances from the get-go proved that he was far from wet behind the ears.

Damaged, but Still Works Well

George Saimes played both safety and running back at Michigan State. And initially, he would do the same with the Bills after being selected in the 1963 AFL draft by the Kansas City Chiefs and then traded to Buffalo. That, however, would come after reporting to Buffalo's training camp with a rib injury that he sustained in the annual Coaches All-America Game.

"It took about five or six weeks to get over that, so I didn't do anything [on the field] for the first three weeks," says Saimes. "So what I was doing was going to the offensive meetings and learning the offense as a running back. Then when I got healthy enough, they had me go to the defensive meetings and learn the safety spot. I was learning two positions! I played the last two exhibition games at safety, but I didn't start. And all of the running backs got hurt over a period of time during the exhibition season."

Because of those injuries, Saimes put attending the defensive meetings on hold for the time being and concentrated on the offensive game plan for the regular-season opener in San Diego.

"Cookie [Gilchrist] started that game, and I'll never forget, I'm on the sideline, and he says, 'Get ready! I may not be able to go.' He played the first series and then came out. He couldn't play! So I played the rest of the game on offense," said Saimes, who rushed for 40 yards on 10 carries against the Chargers. "The second game [at Oakland], I started on offense. And then we came home for the third game against Kansas City, and I went back to the defensive meetings. Back and forth, back and forth. I started the third game at safety"—and intercepted Chiefs quarterback Len Dawson, his first of 22 career picks.

Stealing in Broad Daylight

There's an old tongue-in-cheek adage that cornerbacks are wide receivers who cannot catch. That, however, would not have applied to George "Butch" Byrd. Selected by the Bills in the fourth round of the 1964 AFL draft, the Boston University cornerback arrived in Buffalo with his eyes and ears open.

"Joe Collier, the defensive coach, taught me the strategy, taught all of us the strategy on how to play defense. But the game preparation, how to really one-on-one play cornerback, was Booker Edgerson," said Byrd. "Booker was my mentor. He had been playing, I think, two years. He had a great deal more experience than I did, and he was playing the left corner. He would take me aside and just show me different pointers. I just soaked it up because I didn't want to get cut."

Byrd should not have worried too much about being let go. He started at right cornerback in the season opener against Kansas City, a 34–17 victory. And when the Denver Broncos arrived at War Memorial Stadium a week later, the league's four-time leading wide receiver Lionel Taylor was prepared to test the wet-behind-the-ears rookie. Byrd passed the challenge by holding Taylor to three catches, though one—a pass that Byrd deflected—was for a 16-yard touchdown. Buffalo won, 30–13.

In the first quarter of the third game, at home against San Diego, Byrd collected his first career interception and scored his first career touchdown on the same play. He picked off Chargers quarterback Tobin Rote and returned the ball 75 yards in what would actually turn out to be the game-winning touchdown in the 30–3 victory.

"I owe that one to Booker," says Byrd. "Tobin Rote had a habit. If they were on a drive, at some point he would drop back two or three steps, pump to his right, and then immediately come back and throw to his left side, our right side. They were driving and got pretty close to our 30, and sure enough, he dropped back two steps, pumped it toward Booker, and just automatically threw it back blindly to my side. I saw it all happen and said, 'Well, Booker said this was what was going to happen.' So I stepped in front of it."

Byrd would step in front of six more passes during his rookie campaign and lead the team with seven interceptions. He'd finish his seven-year Bills career as a five-time AFL All-Star and the team's all-time leader with 40 interceptions for 666 yards and five touchdowns.

Making a Cover Corner

Elbert Dubenion not only possessed speed and sure hands as a wide receiver for the Bills during the 1960s, but he was also a valuable college scout for the team after he retired as a player. A case in point is when he spotted Robert James, a 6'1", 188-pound defensive lineman/linebacker at Fisk University, and envisioned him as a defensive back in the pros. In 1970, his second season, James became one of Buffalo's starting cornerbacks and soon thereafter a star in the league.

"Really, my first year there was kind of a learning experience. I had to develop defensive back skills, work on increasing my speed and coverage skills. I focused a whole year just on that right there. Once I developed those skills, then I was able to make the transition," James said. "It was easy in terms of being physical and making contact. The problem was the agility skills of being able to cover some of the fastest guys in football. That's where I had to make an adjustment. I had exceptionally good speed even though I was a lineman; it's just that I didn't know how to use that speed and apply it to my skills. Once I was able to acquire that, then I was able to be competitive as a cornerback in the NFL."

Competitive and then some! James developed into an outstanding cover corner despite having to play for three different head coaches—John Rauch, Harvey Johnson, and Lou Saban—and never winning more than four games per season during the first four years of his career.

"It was kind of a strange experience. I wasn't used to losing. It's not a part of my personality. We went through some losing seasons, and up until Lou Saban came [in 1972], everybody else had had problems trying to put the program together. It was a very hard experience, a very depressing experience," said James, a three-time Pro Bowl selection. "I won't ever forget my second year starting. We only won one ballgame, and that one ballgame really felt like it was the Super Bowl to me, simply because losing was very depressing, and when you work hard and you train hard, you expect to win. You believe you can win. Any game you go in, you play beyond and above your talents and ability. You think that just on your ability that you can win, and I think that's the way every football player should think.

"But in reality, we realize it takes 11 people on the field at the same time giving 100 percent. In the process, they have to be coordinated by a coach. We were falling short somewhere along the way, and we weren't winning, and it was a very depressing experience."

A Rough Start

Buffalo's top draft choice in 1971, J.D. Hill, a wide receiver from Arizona State, experienced a plethora of emotions at the start of his career, beginning with the fourth preseason game on August 29 in Atlanta.

"I was sitting on the bench with [quarterback] James Harris, and I said, 'I wish they'd put us in. We'd show them what we can do!' Just about a minute after that, they called us in," said Hill. "The first pass he threw to me was a 67-yard touchdown pass. We kicked off to them, they fumbled, and the next pass he threw to me was a 69-yard touchdown pass. After the game, I got a message. It said, 'J.D., your mother has died.' So I flew to San Antonio, Texas. I'm embarking upon my career and what have you, I'm excited about things, but emotionally now, I'm wrecked. I buried my mother. I hadn't had any sleep. I had to drive from San Antonio to Dallas, got on an airplane, and flew to Detroit [for the next preseason game]. I met up with the team, and the next night I shouldn't have even played. I hadn't practiced. I was emotionally distraught, and I got my knee tore up and my back hurt.

"I remember running a slant pattern, and I jumped to catch a pass, and [Lions defensive back] Dick LeBeau hit me on my left knee. [Back on the field for a kickoff,] in the process of all the hurry-up and what have you, I went out there and somebody missed a block, and a guy speared me right in the back with his helmet. They carried me off the field, and in the locker room at half-time I hear O.J. [Simpson] saying, 'Let's go out there and get them for Hill.' Well, Buffalo won the game, and I ended up going to the hospital and had my first knee surgery."

After an exhaustive rehabilitation that included getting advice from basketball star Wilt Chamberlain—"Follow everything they tell you to do, but whatever they tell you to do, do a little bit more"—Hill's regular-season debut occurred on November 28, when the 0–10 Bills hosted the Patriots at War Memorial Stadium. The rookie caught three passes for a game-high 82 yards and scored touchdowns of 11 and 47 yards less than six minutes apart in the second quarter. Buffalo won, 27–20, for its only victory that season.

Late-Round Pick to Starting Linebacker

Merv Krakau knew that it was a long shot to even make it through his first training camp with the Bills in 1973 without seeing his name on the league's waiver wire. Selected in the 14th round of the draft, the 344th player chosen overall, the Iowa State defensive end quickly found he would be playing as a linebacker.

"They felt that they wanted a little bit more size as far as height and weight," said the 6'3", 230-pound Krakau. "I think one of the things that really helped me was that I played in the Senior Bowl that year, and the coaches from Buffalo—Lou Saban and his assistants—were the coaches of the North team, which I was on. So they got the opportunity to watch me practice for a week and then play the game and see what I could do. I probably made enough of an impression on them to give me that opportunity."

Having made the roster, when the season opened against New England, Krakau had the unexpected opportunity to be the starting middle linebacker.

"The linebacker that was going to start, Jim Cheyunski, had hurt his knee in a preseason game," Krakau said. "So I had the opportunity and, believe me, it was an experience, because at first you weren't planning on it. To come in and think the chances of making the team were pretty slim and then changing positions and then starting the season opener.... It was a thrill."

And it turned out to be a thrilling game. The Bills won their season opener for the first time in six years by pounding the Patriots, 31–13. Buffalo's O.J. Simpson set an NFL record by rushing for 250 yards, and fullback Larry Watkins added 105 more yards. Meanwhile, Krakau and his defensive teammates held New England's star running back Sam Cunningham to just 53 yards on the ground.

Into the Fire

Much was expected from Mario Clark, an All–Pac Eight corner-back at Oregon and Buffalo's first-round draft choice in 1976. However, being named a starter as a rookie on a team that had just experienced three consecutive winning seasons caught him a little by surprise.

"My first year, they just threw me out there like on-the-job train-ing. I remember that I got burnt a lot of times," said Clark. "On a [season-opening] Monday night game against Miami, [wide receivers] Howard Twilley, Nat Moore, and those guys were having a field day on me. And then I ran into [fullback] Norm Bulaich and got a slight concussion. I was sitting on the bench with my head down, and I'm not knowing this, but [ABC television analyst] Howard Cosell is saying, 'He's just a rookie. He will get better. He is just a rookie.'

"I'd started all my life, even in the All-Star Games, so I just felt like I could start. It was just the mental part of pro football that I really had to get used to. I could have all the physical attributes in the world, but mentally, if I didn't know my plays or if I didn't know the different speeds of the game, then I would be pretty lost. But I had a lot of confidence. I just felt like I could play."

That season, putting it mildly, the Bills did not play very well. More accurately, they were awful. Lou Saban resigned as head coach after five games and was replaced by the team's offensive line coach, Jim Ringo. Under both, Buffalo lost its last 10 games and finished with a 2–12 record, which, oddly enough, was not the worst mark in the NFL, thanks to the first-year Tampa Bay Buccaneers' winless campaign.

"I was kind of used to it because I came from a losing program like Oregon's. I think we won maybe six games [actually 11] in four years. It was something crazy like that, so I didn't know any better," Clark said. "When I got to Buffalo and we started losing, it was kind of like what I was used to. So I always had to make sure my individual game was together.

"Everybody was just trying to survive. We blitzed all the time. Everybody knew what we were doing. I'll never forget when [during a 1977 preseason game, Vikings quarterback] Fran Tarkenton came into our defensive huddle. I was like in awe. It was my second year, and I said, 'God, this is Fran Tarkenton!' I remember the older guys saying, 'Get out of here!' But he came into our huddle and told us, 'You guys can't blitz me.' He even pointed upstairs to whoever the coordinator was at that time, 'Tell your coordinator you guys can't blitz me.' That's just how much disrespect we had at that time."

Not Boxed into a Corner

Talk about having your work cut out for you! Keith Moody arrived at Buffalo's training camp on the Niagara University campus in 1976, not quite in the basement of the cornerbacks depth chart, but let's just say that he was not far from the sump pump. While Moody was selected in the 10th round of the NFL draft out of Syracuse, 280th overall, the Bills' top pick was Oregon cornerback

Mario Clark. And they chose Texas A&M's cornerback Jackie Williams in the seventh round.

"I saw two other DBs before me, and I thought, 'Boy, this is going to be pretty tough,'" said Moody. "And then someone with the organization said, 'Well, they actually need a punt and kick returner, and you do that too. So that's going to give you an inside track on some of the lower-round picks.' That encouraged me and made me glad I did the punt and kick returns in college.

"I looked around and I figured that Dwight Harrison was the corner on one side, and with Mario Clark being the first-round draft choice, I figured they were definitely going to have him there. So at that point, I wanted to make sure I could excel at this area since those two guys were probably shoo-ins. That would at least give me an inside track on other DBs that could be playing the reserve role backing up those two. So I really started to focus on punt and kick returns and wanted to make sure I had a good showing during preseason."

Moody had a good showing during the regular season as well. During that first year, he returned 26 kicks, averaging 23.3 yards per return, and had 16 punts for a 10.4 average, including a 67-yard return for a touchdown against the Jets.

"Punt returns are kind of unpredictable. You never really know what's going to happen. The only thing I can remember is there were a lot of big guys chasing me, and the guys that blocked for me knocked a few of them down. And it was not so much a lot of moves, but just speed," said Moody, who ran a 4.3 40-yard dash. "I got to break to the outside and then just use a lot of speed to get away from them. I didn't have any really great moves, just ran real fast because I was scared."

Less scared the next season, Moody set a team record during the sixth game of the year on October 23, at Rich Stadium against Cleveland, when he returned a punt 91 yards for a touchdown.

"That one was kind of funny because you're not supposed to catch the ball inside the 10. We were instructed to put our heels on the 10 and not back up. I probably took one step backward, and I thought to myself, 'Oh great, I'm going to get yelled at for this one;'" laughed Moody. "The only other thing I can remember on that one was running from one side of the field to the other, and by the time I'd gone 91 yards, I felt like I had run about 250.

"By that second year, I developed a move or two, so I remember faking out one or two guys. And there were some great blocks thrown by Curtis Brown and John Kimbrough that got me going."

Nothing to Lose, Everything to Gain

It did not matter that Shane Nelson was not one of the 335 players chosen during the 1977 NFL draft. The Baylor linebacker would arrive at Buffalo's training camp with the same attitude, whether he was a free agent, which he was, or a first-round selection. "My mind-set pretty much was all or nothing. There was no tomorrow," said Nelson. "As a rookie free agent, you've got to be able to strike quickly as far as getting the coaches to be aware of your talent. You don't come in with any kind of guarantee. Maybe a first- or second-round draft pick has time to develop because they've invested in them. As a rookie free agent, boy, you'd better make things happen quickly to allow coaches to really recognize you. I had nothing to lose, everything to gain."

It is not often that a rookie free agent is acknowledged right away by veterans. The newcomer is trying to take a job from them or their teammates. But Nelson's "nothing to lose, everything to gain" mentality caught the attention of two veterans in the defensive huddle: linebacker John Skorupan and safety Tony Greene. "John really talked to me a lot about the game and helped me become even a better student of the game. He taught me a lot about preparation for a game. In college, you prepared yourself. But it's a whole 'nother level when you really start breaking down game films, understanding tendencies, down, and distance. All that means so much more in the NFL!

"And Tony just was there, just constantly supportive and always encouraging me. He really was instrumental in helping me

Shane Nelson was immediately acknowledged as a stellar player even as a rookie because of his drive and "all or nothing" mentality.

from the standpoint that it gave me somebody to go to. He constantly encouraged me and gave me little tidbits on the field."

While Skorupan and Greene saw something in the young linebacker after he made the Bills roster, opposing running backs did as well—a No. 59 jersey in their faces! Nelson started every game and totaled 168 tackles, earning a place on the NFL's All-Rookie team.

A Quiet Addition

Lucius Sanford and Chuck Knox each made their way to Buffalo in 1978. Knox, the Bills' new head coach, arrived after coaching the Los Angeles Rams to five consecutive division titles. Sanford, an outside linebacker who was selected in the fourth round of that year's NFL draft, came from Georgia Tech, where he led the team in tackles for three straight seasons. Both had a quiet leader personality. And both wanted to achieve the same thing: gridiron success.

"It was not only playing for Knox; it was finally making it to that ultimate dream," said Sanford. "You've been working all your life, trying to walk the straight and narrow and do the right things and listen to the right people, and then all of a sudden, here's this opportunity in front of you to do or die. And then having a coach like Coach Knox coming in, a veteran coach who is supposed to be very good at building a team and that sort, I thought it was a perfect situation for me, in that he's coming in looking to build a team, and I'm new blood coming in. He's basically trying to draft the type of guys he thought that he would need to win.

"I came in and had a really good rookie camp just kind of listening to Tom Catlin, the defensive coordinator and linebacker coach. When he talked, you listened and did those things that he said. And once the veterans came in, I had a decent start and then ended up hurting my shoulder. I think I was out for two weeks with a brace on and not being able to practice. I stayed on the [stationary] bike and did whatever I could. I stayed in the meetings, asked questions, took my notes, and was working really hard. And I did a lot of praying during that time. I did a lot of praying anyway, but the point is, during that time, you didn't know what was coming. But once it healed and I was able to get back in, I remember [assistant coach] Elijah Pitts telling me, 'Hey, you had a really good start coming in, so believe me, we knew that you had a real good chance of making this club.' It worked out for me."

An Invisible Spotlight

It's not often when a team's first-round draft choice—the league's fifth overall pick, no less—is not in the spotlight. But during Buffalo's training camp in 1979, that was the case for wide

Wide receiver Jerry Butler was the Bills first-round draft choice and the league's fifth overall pick in 1979.

receiver Jerry Butler. The reason? He was selected after the Bills' and the NFL's top pick Tom Cousineau, a linebacker Buffalo chose with a draft choice it acquired as part of the O.J. Simpson trade with San Francisco a year earlier.

"In my mind, no matter how I looked at it, I really was a second-round pick in some respects," said Butler. "But I know that I was the fifth pick, and I obviously felt that I had a lot to prove to myself. I think the spotlight was always on Tom Cousineau [who would hold out and never actually play for the Bills]. I kind of got over-looked in that respect, but that's all right. I don't really go for the accolades. I just go do what I need to do."

An admirable attitude, but still, Butler was an All-American at Clemson and the first wide receiver chosen in the draft. Didn't he feel slighted?

"In some respects if you look back, maybe I was. But in the time that I was in it, I didn't feel slighted because I really wasn't an individual that looked for those things," Butler said. "I was more like, where's my next challenge? What do I got to do now?

"In just being in the NFL, having been drafted in the first round, that's still pretty prideful for my family and everything, and that was good enough for me. I really turned my attention to what I need to learn to be the best. My goal was hopefully one day to wind up in Canton." Canton—where members of the Pro Football Hall of Fame wind up.

Tag Team

Barnum and Bailey. Martin and Lewis. A picnic lunch and ants. Some combinations were just destined to be together. The Bills' contribution to that theory was born during the 1979 NFL draft when Fred Smerlas, a nose tackle from Boston College, and Jim Haslett, a linebacker from Indiana University of Pennsylvania, were both selected in the second round.

The two rookies initially became familiar when they each ventured into a hotel game room while in Buffalo for the team's minicamp.

"I brought my girlfriend—five foot, 90 pounds, a real hot-looking girl," says Smerlas. "The buses were coming to take us over to the facility, so I go down to the pinball room, and there's this guy sitting between the two pinball machines like a kid in high school sitting between the sinks having a cigarette. It was Haz! He looked like a bird! A little tiny head, big wide shoulders, and that nose! He was looking at my girlfriend and said, 'Your girlfriend's pretty well-built!' Not quite in those terms. I said, 'What? Who are you?' We almost ended up fighting the first day I met him. Then we started goofing around and became better and better acquainted, and we got to like each other."

They may have liked each other, but they were not the most popular players at the team's training camp—especially among the returning players. Smerlas and Haslett shelved any thoughts of hazing rookies when they turned the tables and began harassing the veterans.

"We did whatever we wanted. We tortured the veterans," Smerlas said. "They were on the downside, so Chuck [Knox] was giving a lot more credit to the rookies. We instantly got all the pub up there, and no one liked pub better than Haz. I saw him tackle a reporter once just to try to get his face on camera."

Once camp ended and the regular season got underway, Smerlas saw Haslett tackling running backs, receivers, and anyone else who may have gotten in the way.

"One thing I did when I was a player, I enjoyed myself off the field, but I worked hard on the field," said Haslett. "I don't know if I would have even started [had Buffalo signed its top draft choice, linebacker Tom Cousineau]. I don't know if I would have been [playing] inside. I probably would have played outside, so I'm sure it would have been a lot different."

Different? Maybe. Less vocal? Doubtful.

"We're lining up on the field, and Haz is talking trash to every-body," Smerlas said. "He's talking trash, grabbing people's face masks, punching people in the stomachs. Just getting everybody all riled up. Of course, I'm the nose tackle, so the first guy they've got to go through is me. So I have to start talking trash. So here are two loud rookies that are talking trash and backing it up! That makes people pissed off.

"And he called his own crap. We had a few fisticuffs on the field because he'd have us move over or run slants [with line calls]. He'd yell, 'Move over!' And I'd yell, 'Shut up!' We just kept yelling back and forth at each other. But in the locker room, as much trash as he talked and as many fights as he got in, Haz was always a student of the game. He'd be in there after everybody went out for a few beers watching film. He'd watch until 2:00 in the morning, breaking it down by plays. He was fanatical. That's what impressed me about Jimmy."

Eager but Cautious

When Tom Cousineau, the first overall selection in the 1979 NFL draft, did not show up at Buffalo's training camp, it opened the door for University of Maine linebacker Chris Keating, who had been undrafted, and he budged right through!

"Jack Bicknell had come from B.C. [Boston College] as an assistant up to Maine as a head coach. He had seen other players go on to the pros and felt that I had a legitimate shot. But kind of hidden in Orono, Maine, it was tough to attract a lot of attention," said Keating. "So when I didn't get drafted, he called several assistant coaches that he knew in the pros and basically gave them his rundown on me. He said that he really thought I had a chance to make it if I got into the right situation, but not to take him into their camps if they're going to take 15 linebackers in already. In other words, who was really looking for linebackers? Several teams said Buffalo. So he called Norm Pollom, who was the director of player personnel. They flew me there the next day, and he and Tom Catlin, the defensive coordinator, worked me out on the field. In all of about 45 minutes, I negotiated my free-agent contract. It wasn't like I had a lot of options."

Considering that the Bills chose Cousineau in the first round and Jim Haslett in the second, it was a fair assumption that they were indeed looking for linebackers. The competition, however, did not dissuade Keating.

"Sometimes what you don't know is great for you. Sometimes ignorance is bliss," he said. "At that point in time, I had no idea what their plans were. Other than Cousineau getting drafted, I had no idea who Jim Haslett even was or whether or not I should be concerned. I just didn't know. I have an older brother who had tried out for the Colts a few years before, and he didn't make out. He really didn't get much of a look either because they were filled at linebackers. So to me it was just get to a situation where I've got a shot.

"My eagerness wasn't low, but my expectations were because I knew what he went through. I knew I might end up getting there and just have a couple of weeks of being a tackling dummy. Luckily they were running an open camp, and it was apparent to me that they were looking for more than just two linebackers."

One Buckeye Who's Happy to Be Here

The telephone in Tim Vogler's Columbus, Ohio, apartment sat silent during the first day of the 1979 NFL draft on May 3. However, the next afternoon during the later rounds, it rang often enough that one would think the Ohio State offensive lineman was taking pledges for a telethon.

"I had people call me and say, 'Hey, we want to sign you as a free agent. We don't feel you're going to get drafted.' About 11 teams did that," laughed Vogler. "Most notably was the Steelers. A bunch of my friends, they're going, 'What do you mean? The Steelers want you to sign; you have to sign with the Super Bowl champions!' But I ended up in Buffalo [who were coming off a 5–11 season]. My friends asked me, 'Why Buffalo over Pittsburgh?' I was like, '[Mike] Webster is the center. How soon do you think he's not going to be playing?' I basically picked the Bills because they weren't a very good team. I thought I had a better opportunity. I was very fortunate. The stories you heard about veterans being kind of aloof or not helping or whatever, when I came in, they had a great bunch of guys: Willie Parker, Joe DeLamielleure, Reggie McKenzie. All those guys were very helpful. Basically, most of their stuff was little techniques. How to step, when to step, what to look for, that kind of stuff. Just things that a few years in the league will teach you."

The following year, Buffalo's head coach Chuck Knox taught Vogler and his teammates how to win. After four consecutive losing seasons and missing the playoffs for five years, the Bills went 11–5 and won the AFC East.

"In our year, they brought in Jerry Butler, Fred Smerlas, [Jim] Haslett, and of course, myself. I was a major contributor," Vogler chuckled. "They finally got some players. In that second year, they got Cribbsy [Joe Cribbs] and [Mark] Brammer, and a few veterans. [Conrad] Dobler came in. And all of a sudden they had a nice mix of talented youth and some veteran players."

Another Target

Through the first nine games of the 1980 season, rookie tight end Mark Brammer had eight receptions for 84 yards and two touchdowns. He made a substantial addition to that total on November 9, when the Bills traveled to New York's Shea Stadium to meet the Jets.

Putting Buffalo on the scoreboard first in the opening quarter after catching a six-yard touchdown pass from Joe Ferguson, Brammer made it 17–0 in the second quarter when he found the end zone on a three-yard toss. The Bills won, 31–24, to improve their record to 7–3, putting them in a tie for the division lead with New England.

"We ended up playing pretty well in that game. I think it did give me a big confidence boost that I could play," said Brammer, Buffalo's third-round draft choice from Michigan State. "Going up against the Jets at that time, they played a 4-3 defense, and I had [defensive linemen Joe] Klecko and [Mark] Gastineau who basically lined up inside of the tight end, and you had to block them. And they were a real load to block! They were two guys that were big and fast. Especially Klecko! He was real powerful and very quick off the line and used his hands well. You just had everything you could do to try to stay connected when you were blocking him."

Brammer did everything he could to keep contributing to the team's success. A reliable target, he finished with 26 catches for 283 yards and four touchdowns. The Bills, with an 11–5 record, earned their first division title since 1966 and had a playoff date (with San Diego) for the first time since 1974.

"It was the first time that Buffalo had made the playoffs in a long time, so there was a lot of excitement in the air. That was the second time that year that we had played San Diego. The first time we played them was our fifth game of the season, and we beat them [26–24]," Brammer said. "Coming back from San Diego and of course, we had gotten back very late at night, I remember there being 4,000–5,000 people at the airport waiting for us. I think that flabbergasted the whole team. There was a huge amount of excitement because of that. I just remember a sea of people.

"Our last game of the season was in San Francisco. We played that game in a mud bowl. And [after] we won there [18–13], we came back to Buffalo, and within the next few days, the coaching staff had planned, because of the weather in Buffalo and everything, to go right back out to California. We practiced at Stanford University for the week, and then we played San Diego [losing 20–14].

"That was a really great experience, just to be able to have that feeling that we've made the playoffs, and the team was playing well and had come together. Coming up to the game, it was just a lot of excitement. The team was really together, and as you know, the outcome wasn't what we all wanted. But unfortunately, with Fergy's ankle injury that he had previously, it was a factor."

Lesson Number One

Linebacker Eugene Marve had a lot to learn about the game after being chosen by Buffalo in the third round of the 1982 NFL draft out of Saginaw Valley State in Michigan. It was not so much about what happens on the field, but more what a rookie should and should not do in the locker room.

"Unfortunately, a reporter had talked to me early in training camp, and I'd had some reasonable success. I didn't start the first preseason game, but I started the second preseason game [against Chicago]," said Marve. "And I got caught in one of those types of questions where I should have humbled myself, but I didn't. They asked me, could I start? And, of course, I said, 'Yes, I can start.' That started kind of like a veteran feud against me in the locker room. Here comes this rookie who starts the second preseason game and then gets in the paper and says he's going to start [the regular season].

"But besides that, I was still fortunate enough to have a friend in the locker room. His name was Booker Moore. Booker was the first-round pick in 1981 and was from the same hometown [Flint, Michigan] that I'm from. So Booker was the one who kind of befriended me. And I'd have to say Sherman White, too. He was an influential guy who helped me through this time. Guys like Fred Smerlas and Jim Haslett were down on me at the time because of my comment in the paper, so I didn't receive too much help from them."

Technically, Marve was not starting at inside linebacker when the regular season opened against Kansas City. He did, however, move into the lineup during the first defensive series against the Chiefs after sixth-year veteran Shane Nelson went out because of an injured knee and remained there for the rest of the season. Finishing second on the team with 63 tackles during the strike-shortened season, Marve was named to the *Football Digest* and *Pro Football Weekly* All-Rookie teams.

"Shane was hurt before the game, and I really respected Shane," Marve said. "He didn't practice much during training camp. He never recovered from his [previous season's] knee injury. The last week before the season opener, he was trying to come back, and he would pull me to the side and encourage me, and he'd tell me to be ready to play. He didn't think he'd be able to go the distance in that game. And, unfortunately, he didn't go very far."

A Diamond in the Rough

Twelve wide receivers were selected in the 1985 NFL draft before Buffalo chose Kutztown (Pennsylvania) University's Andre Reed in the fourth round. But only two, San Francisco's Jerry Rice and Cincinnati's Eddie Brown, both first-round selections, would catch more passes during their rookie seasons.

Reed, actually, was not even the first wide receiver chosen by the Bills that year. Chris Burkett was a second-round pick. Even so, Reed knew very early on that he had what it takes to make the team.

Pictured here in 1985, soon after being drafted as a fourth-round pick by the Buffalo Bills, Andre Reed caught the third-most passes of any NFL rookies that season.

"I think it was the first day of training camp. The Bills that year had drafted not only me, but two other receivers," said Reed. "They drafted a guy in the second round, a guy in the fifth round [Jimmy Teal], and I was in the fourth round. So there was a lot of competition in camp. A lot of free agents! I think there might have been 16 or 17 receivers in camp. Back then you could stack it up like that at certain positions.

"I remember catching a pass from Vince Ferragamo. It was a deep-in route, and I came across the middle and the ball was a little bit high, so I had to jump for it. The safety hit me right under my legs, and I kind of got flipped a little bit and landed on my back. I got up and went back to the huddle. I knew from there not only that I belonged, but that I could be an impact and play. I think it was just that play. There were probably a lot of them, but for a 21-year-old kid coming from a small school, I think in the beginning of training camp, the first day, that sure opened up a lot of eyes."

It didn't take long before he was opening a lot of eyes around the league. Starting 15 of 16 games, Reed caught at least one pass in all but one game and finished with 48 receptions (second to running back Greg Bell) for 637 yards and four touchdowns. The rookie also learned firsthand that the NFL is a business. After the Bills lost their first four games by a combined score of 100–46, head coach Kay Stephenson was replaced by Hank Bullough. The coaching change did not alter the Bills' momentum, however, and they finished with a dismal 2–14 record.

"As a rookie, I just wanted to play. That was the big thing for me," Reed said. "I just wanted to show that being drafted in the fourth round, I belonged there. Of course the records did mean a lot to me, but I think at the same time, I just wanted to contribute as much as I could. At that time, the Bills were [starting] their rebuilding years, and I wanted to be a part of that rebuild.

"The coaches were changing and the players were changing and the organization was changing to a certain point, so it was tough. But again, just being on an NFL roster and being able to play and contribute probably was the biggest thing for me."

Reed would certainly go on to make big contributions. Huge, in fact! Over 15 seasons with the Bills, he would total 941 receptions for 13,095 yards and 86 touchdowns. All team records! And he contributed in the playoffs, as well. One example: in the 1992 AFC Wild Card Game against Houston—otherwise known as the greatest comeback in NFL history—after Buffalo rallied from a 32-point deficit to win 41–38 in overtime, he had eight catches for a game-high 136 yards and three touchdowns.

Reed feels that any success he accomplished on the field was because he was prepared.

"Year after year, I was able to get myself ready for training camp, get myself ready for the season, play at a high level, and try to play better than the previous year," said the seven-time Pro Bowl selection. "The individuals on our team at that time, I think everybody had that attitude. We wanted to be better! That's one of the things that I pride myself in, just being prepared every season and being prepared every game."

From Linebacker U. to Orchard Park

Two games into the 1987 season and his NFL career, linebacker Shane Conlan put away his shoulder pads, reached for a picket sign, and joined the rest of his teammates in a league-wide players strike. But after such a brief time with the team, was it difficult to understand just why they were protesting?

"Yeah, it was," said the first-round draft choice from Penn State. "Because I think when you're young, you see paychecks, you're playing, you're having fun, and then they say we're not going to do this. But back then, we wouldn't even think about going in and playing [i.e., crossing the picket line] because you had the older guys like the Fred Smerlases, the Joe Devlins, that said, 'Listen, you're not going anywhere. You're staying with us.' So it was a pretty easy decision to make."

Shortly after the players and owners settled their differences, the Bills were involved in a three-team trade with Indianapolis and the Los Angeles Rams, which brought another rookie linebacker—the second overall pick, Cornelius Bennett—to One Bills Drive. The two first-round selections were now not only on the same team but on the field at the same time as well.

"It was different. I remember the first time, one of the inside linebackers went down and Cornelius came running on. Because he was playing behind me at the time, I started to go out and he said, 'No, you go inside.' I said, 'I don't know how to do this.' But I remember talking to our defensive coordinator, Walt Corey, and he said, 'Just tackle the guy with the ball.' So I just ran around. It was fun. That first year was great."

That it was. The Frewsburg, New York, native led the Bills with 114 tackles and was named the NFL's Defensive Rookie of the Year by the Associated Press.

Introducing Dependability

If a rookie can play, it really does not matter whether he arrives in Buffalo from a college football powerhouse such as USC, Ohio State, or Texas. Or in the case of Phil Hansen, from defending Division II champion North Dakota State.

After being selected in the second round of the 1991 NFL draft, Hansen found himself filling in for an injured Bruce Smith in the Bills' starting lineup in only his second game, against Pittsburgh on September 8. "I'm sure I was nervous, but I was up for the challenge. I was finding my way, I guess you'd say. I was finding what would work for me and what wouldn't," said Hansen, who would make 10 starts as a rookie and total 40 tackles and two sacks. "I had a great supporting cast. When they talked amongst themselves, I'm sure they said, 'Aw jeez, we've got to cover for him.' Which they pretty much did, but they never made me feel that way. They always accepted me and made me feel like I was a part of their unit. And once we got out there and the bullets were flying for real on the field, it didn't matter. It was us against them. And I was improving. They could see improvement week to week."

Week to week became year to year. And in 11 seasons, Hansen—who became the starting left defensive end, played in 156 games and had 876 total tackles, 133 quarterback pressures, 61.5 sacks, and one touchdown—scored against the Raiders in 1998 on a 13-yard fumble recovery. Although admired and consistent in the eyes of Buffalo's coaches, players, and fans, because Smith was at the other end of the line, Hansen may not have received the national recognition he deserved.

"No, I'm very happy with my career," said Hansen. "You know, you could look at that several different ways. When people looked at our defense and looked at our defensive line, Bruce Smith was the first thing that came to mind. So maybe I got lost in the numbers and they didn't account for me as much. I don't think that was a bad thing. Do I think I got overshadowed? I got a lot of good publicity. I would have loved to go to a Pro Bowl, which I never got to do. But was that because of Bruce Smith? No, that was because I didn't play well enough to go to a Pro Bowl.

"I was never the greatest player on the field, but what I gave to the Bills, I want to be remembered as a consistent, dependable, and accountable football player. Someone who the coaches always knew where I was and what they'd get out of me week in and week out. I had an 86-game, five-year starting streak. I'm proud of that! Eighty-six games over the span of five years! A lot of those things, they followed me from youth, and they'll follow me for the rest of my life. I'm dependable. I'm accountable. I'll stand up if I make a mistake. You won't have to worry about me shifting the blame. It's my mistake and I'll fix it. I was always consistent. A lot of coaches were very happy with, 'Well, he may not be the best player in the world, but at least we know what we get with Phil Hansen. He may not be in the line of Bruce Smith, but he's not going to let us down. He's going to give us everything he has.'"

Northern Exposure

With a veteran defense including Bruce Smith, Ted Washington, and Phil Hansen up front along with Bryce Paup and Chris Spielman at linebacker, it did not appear that rookie Gabe Northern would be on the field for much more than pregame calisthenics and special teams.

That, however, abruptly changed when the second-round draft pick from LSU found himself in the Bills' huddle during the first series against Indianapolis on October 6, 1996. Third-year outside linebacker Sam Rogers sprained his knee on Buffalo's first defensive play and headed up the Rich Stadium tunnel to the locker room while Northern headed out onto the field.

"When you go out to the game, you don't really expect anybody to get hurt. And you don't want anybody to get hurt," said Northern. "I just wanted to go out there and do whatever I could. I thought Sam would be right back out."

While Rogers was unable to return, Colts quarterback Jim Harbaugh was unable to ignore the 6'2", 240-pound rookie. Thinking about testing the new guy? Think again. To go along with eight tackles and three quarterback pressures, Northern notched the first two sacks of his career. The first, in the third quarter, could not have come much easier. Instead of taking a direct hit from Northern, Harbaugh hit the turf for an 11-yard loss.

"I really hadn't pictured getting a sack in that game, but I guess he just made it easier for me," Northern said. "It was a smart play on his part because he would have lost yardage anyway with the intentional grounding. There was nobody to throw to."

The two would meet in Indianapolis's backfield again during overtime. On a second down and eight at the Colts 16-yard line, Northern raced past Harbaugh's protection and threw him down for a seven-yard loss. They punted after the next play, and the Bills were able to drive for a 39-yard game-winning field goal, 16–13.

"As far as the sacks go, I think it was the luck of the draw," said Northern. "Rogers went down early in the game, and I think if he was in, he'd have done the same thing."

Northern's veteran teammates were impressed after he followed his performance against the Colts with two splendid starts against Miami and the New York Jets while Rogers recuperated.

"I'm very happy with the way Gabe has come in and performed," said defensive end Bruce Smith. "I think he's doing an outstanding job. The fact that he's been able to come in and make an impact for this football team and do the things that he's capable of doing is just a plus for the team."

chapter 3
Coming...

Pete Metzelaars, pictured here in 1989, was disappointed that he was traded from the Seattle Seahawks to the Buffalo Bills, arguably the worst team in the NFL at the time.

It's a Business

Fourth-year veteran offensive tackle Dave Foley was reminded during the 1972 training camp with the New York Jets that, at times, the NFL can be a cold business.

"They brought in a new line coach, and I wasn't getting along with the guy, so I knew that I wasn't going to have a shot at playing there because he and I were not seeing eye to eye as far as what his expectations were and what my abilities were," said Foley. "As a matter of fact, they brought in another tackle, Bob Svihus, from Oakland, and immediately he was the starting left tackle. Having that experience, I knew that the writing was on the wall. They worked me a lot at center, and I tried other positions, and it just wasn't working out. So the best thing that could possibly happen to me was getting out of New York, because I wasn't going to play there."

That possibility became a reality when the Jets placed Foley on waivers. "That was kind of an interesting story. On the last day of summer camp I went into the training room because I had gotten hurt the week before. The trainer came in and said, '[Head coach] Weeb Ewbank said you've got to leave.' So I get up and leave. They're playing Buffalo the next week and putting in the game plan that day. I figured I was gone, but I didn't figure I was necessarily going to Buffalo. So I go home, and all my buddies came over after their practice, and we're having a few beers, just kind of relaxing on the porch, and the phone rings. I pick up the phone, and a guy says, 'Hey, this is Coach. When can you get here?' I said, 'Coach who? And get where?' Nobody ever told me what the deal was. Then he said, 'This is Lou Saban. You're now on the Buffalo Bills. When can you get to Buffalo?' That's the way things happen in the NFL. You just never know."

With Mixed Emotions

Trades between division rivals are not too common. But in 1973, the Bills sent reserve fullback Wayne Patrick and linebackers

Edgar Chandler and Jeff Lyman to the Patriots for middle line-backer Jim Cheyunski, defensive end Halvor Hagen, and offensive lineman Mike Montler.

Cheyunski, a Massachusetts native who was entering his sixth season, arrived in Buffalo having never experienced a winning record. "My family was there and everything, but the team was absolutely horrible. So I guess it was kind of a mixed emotion," said Cheyunski. "Defensively, we never got off the field, and I took a physical beating because of that. When I beat [Nick] Buoniconti out [for the starting middle linebacker position], I wish they [the Patriots] would have traded me instead of him because he went on to some Super Bowls [with Miami], and I went on to some knee operations. We had a rough time there. We didn't win many ball-games. It was nice to get out of there, but they were just bringing Chuck Fairbanks in [as head coach], who I thought might be able to turn the situation around. But going to the Bills, I knew that I had to try and win a spot again, and I was fairly confident of that."

Having won the spot during training camp, Cheyunski was all set to play under his fifth head coach in the NFL, Lou Saban. "He surprised me a little bit because he's an ex-linebacker, so you'd think he would have been very, very much defensive-minded. I really didn't find him to be that way. I think, pretty much, that O.J. Simpson and the boys on offense ran the whole show up there. Of course, it's to be expected. They put a lot of points on the board. But what people didn't realize, we also had one of the better defenses in the NFL during those years. We had a pretty good group of people. I think they found that out when they started trading some of the defensive people away.

"Lou was a tough guy, and I liked that type of hard, strong dis-cipline, but I kind of wish that maybe the defense had gotten a little bit more credit, number one. And I also wish that maybe we threw the ball a little bit more because I think that would have helped O.J. get even more yardage if we mixed it up a little bit. Joe Ferguson, I had all the respect in the world for him because he was an excel-lent quarterback, but he really didn't get too much of a shot to throw."

The Surprised Man in the Middle

There is no question that the more things a player can do, the more valuable he is to a team. But there are times when a player can be more valuable than he even knows. Mike Montler spent four seasons with the Patriots, making 50 starts at offensive guard and tackle, before he became part of a six-player trade with the Bills on April 19, 1973. He arrived in Buffalo not knowing that he'd soon begin playing at yet another position and become the team's starting center.

"I went there to play tackle. At the time, Buffalo did not even have a left tackle," said Montler. "I thought this was automatic. That's why they brought me to Buffalo, to move me to that left tackle spot. When I did get to Buffalo, the equipment man handed me my jersey and it was a 50s number. This was a little bizarre because I had never played center before in my life. I said, 'What's going on here with this? I think you made a mistake.' He said, 'No, the coaching staff told me that you're to have a 50s number.' Back then, they really adhered to the numbering system of 50s being a center, 60s for guards, and 70s for tackles. So then they informed me that I was going to be a center, which didn't make me real happy.

"It basically amounted to someone gambling with my career, other than the fact that they were not happy with their current center because he had a tendency to get hurt too often. I'd watch Bruce Jarvis on film, and I'd say, 'My God, this guy is a great center! What's going on? You've got a 29-year-old backing up a 23-year-old? That doesn't bode well for a guy like myself.' They just said, 'Hang in there.' Back then, you were much more disciplined. You didn't question authority. You just kind of hung in there and hung in there, and eventually he got banged up a couple times, and I went in. When he came back, they said, 'Never mind.'"

Put Right to Work

It is generally not going to be a good day for a young football player when he is told by his head coach, "That's the way it goes, son. It's a big business." But that's what Miami's Don Shula said to Mike Kadish on August 28, 1973, when the second-year defensive tackle was traded from the defending Super Bowl champions to Buffalo, who were coming off a 4–9–1 year, for offensive lineman Irv Goode. "What he said was that they needed to make some moves on the Dolphins' offensive line," says Kadish. "[Bills coach] Lou Saban had seen me play in an exhibition game that was on national TV. They worked out some kind of deal, and I was off to Buffalo."

Having spent his rookie season on the taxi squad, Kadish watched his teammates compile the NFL's only undefeated season and was looking to help the Dolphins defend their title.

"It was not exactly something that I was all that excited about, to tell you the truth," Kadish said of the trade. "I got into Buffalo and [Bills scout] Elbert Dubenion picked me up at the airport and took me to Rich Stadium, which was new at the time. I went up to Coach Saban's office, and my first duty as a Buffalo Bill was to assist Elbert in going over to Ilio DiPaolo's [restaurant] and picking up chicken wings and pizza for the coaching staff."

It Was One of Those Days

Just ask Lou Piccone. Some days stand out much more than others. For him it was August 31, 1977. Less than three weeks before what would have been the start of his fourth season with the New York Jets, the wide receiver walked out of the team's training facility unaware of how much his life would change in just a matter of minutes.

"I had talked with the Jets organization at the time, and it seemed to be that I was pretty solid. I was sort of assured that I was okay," said Piccone. "I finally had a little bit of extra cash and went out and bought a used Corvette. And that morning it was missing! I thought somebody was pulling my chain. I was rooming with Marty Domres, the quarterback, and Marty was a prankster. So I went out and looked around, and nobody had seen it, so I went and reported it stolen.

"While I'm sitting there, [head coach] Walt Michaels comes out and says, 'Lou, I'm really sorry to hear about your car being stolen, and you've been traded to Buffalo.' It was all one sentence! Walt never minced words. He had gone from defensive coordinator to head coach that year, and with him being on the defensive side of the ball, you really didn't have too many conversations with Walt. But that just blew me away. My car was stolen and I got traded to Buffalo."

This was not the first experience Piccone had had that involved the Bills. "In 1974 we played there, and it snowed and sleeted, the temperatures dropped to subfreezing, and the water backed up on the field," Piccone said. "There wasn't a pass completed until the last quarter. [Joe] Namath threw a five-yard out to David Knight, and it ended up 25 yards behind the line of scrimmage. The weather was so bad, so ugly, so cold. We were standing in probably four or five inches of water. It just chilled to the bone. I remember saying to myself, 'God, don't ever let me be traded up here.' I must have done something wrong because the year [before] I got traded up to Buffalo, the Jets won three games. We beat the Bills twice and Tampa Bay once. The Bills were our highlight film. But coming here ended up being a good move career-wise from the standpoint that I did get a lot of playing time."

Quite a Catch

It's generally viewed as a positive move when an NFL team can trade for a quality player with Super Bowl experience that has his best seasons ahead of him. The Bills acquired just that type of individual from the Pittsburgh Steelers in August 1978 in veteran wide receiver Frank Lewis.

"I wasn't expecting to go to Buffalo. My first reaction was if I'm going to be traded, hopefully, it would be to a warm-weather team," said the Houma, Louisiana, native. "Since I had been playing my whole career in the cold weather and on turf, I was hoping that if it would happen, to go to warm weather with some grass. But once it was done, it didn't make any difference. It's a matter of if a team would like for you to play for them, then that's where you want to be anyway.

"He [Chuck Knox] expected me to come in and give some productivity for him. It wasn't like I had a role. He was in need of a receiver. He looked at me as a veteran receiver because I had been playing for seven years. He had a few guys hurt and a young group, so he just needed a little bit more stability. I was the guy who had been around the longest, except for Bobby Chandler, but I think Bobby was hurt at the time."

In an ironic twist, Buffalo opened its regular season against the Steelers at Rich Stadium. Lewis caught two passes for 46 yards, including a 22-yard touchdown reception from Bill Munson in the 28–17 loss.

"Pittsburgh was a team that was supposed to come in and win the game, but we almost [beat them]," Lewis said. "The Bills had so many new players at the time it was just hard to compete against a team that was that established. Pittsburgh went on to win the Super Bowl that year, so they were strong. We were just on our way of building. But it was just another game, and my main concern was to try to fit into Buffalo's system."

Paying the Dues

No one has to tell Steve Freeman about having to pay your dues. After being selected by the Patriots in the 1975 NFL draft, the defensive back was released and ended up in Buffalo's training camp after just two preseason games. Once with the Bills, his focus was on establishing himself through special teams.

"When you're coming in as a rookie you've got to play all the special teams to make the club," said Freeman. "Back then, we didn't have much nickel coverage. The nickel coverage stuff didn't really come in until the late '70s, so it was a question of a 42-man roster. How do you make it? You make it as a backup. If not a backup, come in there and start. What the heck? But if you're not going to start, you play special teams. You play them all."

Freeman played them all and served as a backup until he earned the starting strong-safety spot midway through the 1978 campaign.

"I probably wasn't totally prepared to start at first, which a lot of rookies aren't. There's so much to learn," Freeman said. "I started as a rookie my first six games of the year before Tony Greene came off the injury list. I played okay, but I made some rookie mistakes that you're going to make. And the only way you're going to learn is generally by making a mistake so you don't make it again. So I didn't feel pressed to be a starter and wasn't just yearning to be a starter until I had learned what I think I needed to learn at my position. Fortunately, I was given the time to do that.

"A lot of times you're not given that opportunity to learn before they cut you. The average deal is not but about three years in the league. You can't learn anything that you need to learn in those years. You've got to have the experience. I had the opportunity to gain that experience before I became a starter."

Two seasons after achieving that position, Freeman led the Bills with seven interceptions after collecting six during his first five years. What clicked for him? "Great coaches. Great players. We had a scheme that year. Tom Catlin was our coordinator. Jim Wagstaff was our secondary coach. He was one of those guys that when you play for him, you don't want to let him down. You're going to go out there and play your best," said Freeman. "The scheme that we ran put us in situations to make interceptions. I could have had a couple more that year and led the league. I think [Oakland's] Lester Hayes led the league that year. I dropped two or three that would have put me right up there with him. It was just a situation of learning the system, learning where to be, learning what everybody else on defense was doing, and having confidence in your abilities to make plays. That's really all it was."

Advice from Mr. Davis

One thing that linebacker Phil Villapiano learned during his nine seasons with Oakland was that if Raiders owner Al Davis offers advice, listen! Even if it's during a telephone conversation to inform you that you've been traded to Buffalo. "'Phil, it's going to work out fine for you,'" Villapiano recalls Davis telling him in April 1980. "'Chuck Knox really wants you. They need an experienced linebacker. Go there with a good attitude, and everything is going to turn out perfect.'"

Phil Villapiano was not initially happy about being traded to the Bills from the Raiders, but he soon came to appreciate the Bills' enthusiasm and athleticism and played a large part in pulling them out of their slump.

Considering the Bills had just gone through their fourth consecutive losing season, Villapiano could have been at least a little skeptical of Davis's parting words. He, however, felt better about the situation soon after reporting to minicamp. "My biggest memory of when I got to Buffalo was the size of the guys. Joe Devlin, Kenny Jones, Reggie McKenzie—they were all big, but they were all cut," said Villapiano, who was traded to the Bills for wide receiver Bobby Chandler. "The Raiders were all big, but they were just big. Not cut like these guys. I remember sitting there with Conrad Dobler saying, 'Connie, look at these young guys. These guys are in shape!' And they were! Everybody was lifting weights, trying to make their bodies bigger and stronger, where in Oakland, nobody lifted weights. It was a different, more modern-type team than the Raiders were.

"One other thing I noticed besides that was how many really good players were in Buffalo. The only thing they needed was what Chuck Knox did: bring in some old guys to help out the young guys. The young guys were great athletes. They just didn't know they were. I remember sitting with Reggie [McKenzie] and Joe Ferguson and Roosevelt Leaks and Ron Jessie and Frank Lewis and Conrad and Isiah Robertson, and saying, 'Hey, man, I know we've got a real good team here. Why don't we win?' Everybody just said, 'Yeah, let's not be a 2–14 team. Let's win!' We had a real good blend of people. The talent was excellent! Much better talent in Buffalo than in Oakland. All Buffalo needed was just a little fine tuning in the mental sect."

You Just Never Know

Timing is everything! He was in the right place at the right time! Either of these clichés could be used to describe how in 1980, five-year veteran free safety Bill Simpson joined his former coaches Chuck Knox and Jim Wagstaff in Buffalo.

He had actually been traded to the Bills from the Rams a year earlier but didn't pass the physical because of a collection of knee injuries. So after taking the 1979 season off to get healthy, on October 5, 1980, Simpson took a trip from his home in Los Angeles to San Diego to watch the Bills take on the Chargers. Buffalo won the game that afternoon; however, they lost free safeties Rod Kush and Jeff Nixon, who was leading the NFL in interceptions, to season-ending knee injuries.

"It was probably the most unique situation you'll ever run across," Simpson said. "After the game, I was talking to Coach Wagstaff, and he said, 'How are you feeling?' I said, 'I feel good. I feel darn good.' And he said, 'Don't be surprised if you get a call later on tonight.' I said, 'Are you serious?' He said, 'Yeah. We need a safety and you know the system. I'm going to talk to Chuck and see what he has to say and talk to the owner, Ralph Wilson, and see if we can get something done.' And lo and behold, later that night I got a call. He said, 'What do you think?' I said, 'Hey, I'm willing to take a shot at it. Why don't we see if we can't get something done?'"

Fortunately for Simpson, Buffalo was running basically the same defense that Knox and his staff had used in Los Angeles. That helped a lot considering that only three days after joining the Bills and more than 21 months since the last time he stepped onto a field, Simpson was playing in an NFL game. And starting, no less!

"I was glad to be back in an organization that had a great season going. It was a real positive situation," said Simpson. "Yeah, there were butterflies. The speed of the game is something that you're never quite sure how you're going to react to once you get in there, but I felt real good, real comfortable. After the first quarter, I felt right at home. I felt like I had never left the field. A couple of things had been tweaked. A little bit different here, a little bit different there, but the basics of it were the same. When you play in a system for a while, you can pick it up pretty quick. Even the little nuances of it. That's one reason, I think, that Coach Wagstaff and Coach Knox wanted to get someone in that knew the system, so they didn't have to retrain somebody and that type of thing."

Simpson knew the system, and in that first game, with seven tackles and an interception, he proved he also knew where to be on the field. He finished the season with three more interceptions and helped lead the Bills to their first playoff appearance in six years.

Don't Judge a Book...

In 1984 the Chuck Knox–led Seattle Seahawks, at 12–4, compiled the best record of their nine-year-old life. That same season, the Bills won just two of 16 games under Kay Stephenson, who had succeeded Knox in Buffalo. Their worst record in 13 years! They were two teams whose immediate futures were heading in opposite directions.

Just three weeks before the 1985 season got underway, fourth-year veteran tight end Pete Metzelaars found himself heading in the less attractive direction. Traded to the Bills for wide receiver Byron Franklin, he questioned the route his career was taking.

"I wasn't real happy," said Metzelaars. "I guess I was somewhat naïve going into it, thinking that I was going to play my whole career in Seattle. And then to have that happen, it was kind of like a big slap in the face. So it was a difficult transition and a little frustrating. And then also the point of going from a team that many were predicting was going to the Super Bowl to a team that was arguably the worst team in the league, I was like, 'Oh gosh, not there of all places.'"

Starting off the 1985 campaign with four losses, the Bills replaced Stephenson with defensive coordinator Hank Bullough. But by winning just two games during the rest of the season to finish with back-to-back 2–14 records, the coach was the only change in Buffalo.

"I'm going, 'What did I get myself into? A new coach! A whole new situation! What's going on with it and what do I do? How do I fit into this?' I started often early in the year, and then I ended up getting benched the second half of the season, so that doubled the frustration of the whole thing," Metzelaars said. "I'm going, 'Gosh, I can't even play, and I can't start on arguably the worst team in the league? What's going to happen to me? Where am I going to go? Am I even going to be able to have a career? Am I going to be able to play?' All those kinds of things were flying through my mind."

These questions began to be answered the following season when Marv Levy became the head coach and Metzelaars became a large part of the offense. His role increased, and he left the Bills after the 1994 season as the team's fourth all-time leading receiver with 302 catches and 25 touchdowns.

A Rookie with Experience

One thing that certainly can be said about Ray Bentley is that when he arrived in Buffalo two games into the 1986 season, he was already experienced.

The inside linebacker had played three seasons in the recently disbanded USFL—two with the Michigan Panthers and one with the Oakland Invaders—and he had participated in that year's Tampa Bay Buccaneers training camp.

"I lasted until the final cuts, and they let me go, which was a blessing," said Bentley. "At that point, I didn't know what I was going to do. I went up to Montreal for a tryout [with the CFL's Alouettes], and Marv Levy was there as a consultant. He had been their coach and had won several Grey Cups. And I had also talked with the Bills. Hank Bullough was the coach at the time, and Hank had been my father's coach at Michigan State, so he knew the family and also knew me from the USFL because he had coached with the Pittsburgh team.

"Hank said, 'I don't have a spot for you right now, but if something happens, I'm going to bring you here.' So I told Marv that I had to see what happened with the Bills before I could sign with those guys. And it happened that Mark Kelso got injured [during the second game], and they had a roster spot, so they signed me. The other part of that story: When Marv came in as coach [of the Bills after nine games that season], he said, 'Well, you wouldn't come up to Montreal with me, so I had to come to Buffalo to be with you.' I'd been playing special teams and just getting a few downs here and there, but as soon as Marv came in, he moved me right into the starting lineup."

Bentley was not the only former USFL player who was starting for the Bills. Quarterback Jim Kelly had firsthand knowledge of the linebacker's on-field tenacity. Bentley was with Michigan when they faced Kelly on the Houston Gamblers. "We played the Houston Gamblers in an overtime game, and we beat them," recalled Bentley. "And there was actually some controversy because they had a center by the name of Frank Kalil, who spit in my face during the game. So I went over after the game and got into a fight with him. And Kelly, in the paper, was saying what a cheap-shot artist I was and all this stuff. So my first day in the Bills locker room, I went over to him and said, 'You still think I'm a cheap shot?' We had a good laugh over that."

Nice to Meet You

The NFL players' strike that began on September 21, 1987, a day after the Bills beat the Houston Oilers to even their record at 1–1, offered a unique opportunity for Scott Radecic. Having been claimed off waivers from Kansas City less than a week before the season opened, the linebacker had not gotten to know his new teammates all that well.

"It was an awkward situation just to be on strike, but that time really allowed me to get to know a lot of the other players. We would have unofficial practices at various locations around town. It was pretty beneficial," said Radecic. "It was good from my standpoint because [former Chiefs coach] Walt Corey had come in [as Buffalo's defensive coordinator] and installed a new defensive scheme. Well, it was the same defense we'd played in Kansas

City, so I knew the scheme better than those guys did. It worked out where we were able to share information and develop some relationships. So even though it was awkward from the standpoint [of], yeah, we were on strike, it was a good opportunity to get to know people in, at that time, a nonthreatening way. It's not like we're practicing and anybody is challenging anybody. We were all just trying to stay in shape and be ready for when the strike was over."

Radecic had yet another teammate to get to know soon after the strike ended when the Bills acquired rookie linebacker Cornelius Bennett as part of a three-team deal with the Colts and Rams.

"That was awesome. Getting Cornelius was one of the best things that we could have done as a defense because of what he was able to do in college, his ability as a rush end and as an athlete. We were looking to add that to the team," Radecic said. "My primary position was inside linebacker, and they were bringing in Cornelius as an outside linebacker, so I didn't feel threatened in any way because we did two different things. But as time went on, I had kind of taught myself how to play outside linebacker just in case there was ever any problem. And I guess it was the next year, we ended up having some injury problems. So my being able to play any position, I was able to contribute much more to the success of the team whether I was where Cornelius would be or where Darryl [Talley] would play or I would play or Shane [Conlan] would play or whatever. I think we had the best linebacking corps in the NFL for those two or three years."

Could Still Do the Job

During the 1988 season opener against Minnesota, 11-year veteran defensive end Art Still showed just why the Bills traded for him three months earlier. Playing without defensive end Bruce Smith, who was suspended for four weeks by the NFL under its substance abuse program, Still recorded two and a half sacks as

Buffalo beat the Vikings, 13–10, starting a four-game winning streak. The Bills went on to finish the season with a 12–4 record and advanced to the AFC Championship Game, their first trip to a title game since the AFL Championship Game 22 years earlier.

"I think we played in one playoff game during my [10] years in Kansas City, and then coming up there my first year and making it to the AFC Championship Game...and we had a chance at winning that," said Still. "There was nothing but talent on the team. You had a combination of young players, players who'd been around for a little bit, and seasoned players. Plus, there was a bond. When we played the game, it was fun. That's what we made it, fun! We won games. There were some tight games, but we had that mental capability as far as wanting the game, even when you're down. It was just a good feeling within the organization, the players working together as a family.

"Throughout that whole season, it was a special bond. There's only so much you can do in a game. You're going to make mistakes, that's a given. There hasn't been anybody who has played a perfect game. But you go out there and play the best that you can, and you have other ballplayers with that same mentality out there. Everybody supported one another. Mistakes will happen, but you've got ballplayers saying, 'Hey, that's all over. Let's keep rolling.' That's the type of environment, no matter if it's on the field or off the field, you enjoy being around."

Plan B was K.D.

Elijah Pitts was a standout player, a terrific coach, and when Kenneth Davis showed up at Rich Stadium during the 1989 Plan B free-agency period, he proved to be an outstanding recruiter as well. His candor attracted and impressed the fourth-year running back.

"I think coming in and talking with him, he was being real honest with me and frank about what was going on and where the organization was trying to go with their athletes," said Davis, who

Running back Kenneth Davis runs with the ball during a 21–11 victory over the Miami Dolphins at Rich Stadium in Orchard Park, New York, on October 9, 1994. Davis was attracted to the Bills by the candor and honesty of recruiter Elijah Pitts.

had spent the previous three seasons with Green Bay. "And letting me know that he did have other guys that were ahead of me [on the depth chart]. He would give me an opportunity to compete, but also an opportunity to contribute to a team that he felt was going to do a lot of great things.

"He didn't mention any specific role [I would play with the Bills]. He just told me that he felt that we had a good, young team that was going to be successful and that I could be an integral part of that success. He didn't know how much or how little. That's something that he couldn't promise me. He said that those opportunities would be left up to me."

Davis accepted Buffalo's offer and joined the team, which had just made it to the AFC Championship Game and had a solid running back in Thurman Thomas, who would be entering only his second season. Certainly, he knew he would be second string, but with his attitude, that did not bother him.

"To be able to have an individual come off the bench and go in there and make some plays and make some things happen, that's part of being successful," Davis said. "You've got to be able to do what it takes to win by being a starter or a backup. I came off the bench, but I always prepared as a starter. I didn't look at it any other way because I felt that when it was my time to go into the game, I was the starter! That's the only way to look at it. You have to go in there and give your best because you don't know what play is going to be the key play to win or lose the ballgame."

Proving His Worth

After 11 seasons in the NFL, compiling 599 catches for 11,085 yards and 54 touchdowns, seven-time Pro Bowl wide receiver James Lofton was all but assured a place in the Hall of Fame following his career. However, even with those statistics, Lofton still had to show the Bills he could play before they signed him as a free agent on September 26, 1989, two days after winning their second game in the young season.

"After getting released by the Raiders, I was 33, and a lot of people just figured I was done playing, didn't want to play anymore," said Lofton. "But nothing could have been further from the truth. I came in for a tryout with two other receivers. They sounded like they wanted to go with an experienced guy, so I was really the lucky one in the deal. Like anybody coming to a new team, the first thing you have to do is try and catch up and learn the offense. Nobody ever sat down and said, 'You know, you have a chance to be a starter here.' I just came in and tried to catch up as quickly as possible."

Lofton finished the season with eight catches for 166 yards and three touchdowns. He added three receptions for 66 yards, including a 33-yard touchdown in the Wild Card Game loss in Cleveland.

"It's funny, when I look back at just that one season, things were going by so quickly. They were in a playoff race; the team had started to stagger a little bit, so they were trying to get themselves straightened out," Lofton said. "There wasn't a lot of time to just sit around and do nothing. You went in and you worked hard. I was able to get into some games late in the season, do a little bit, and then got to play in the playoff game against Cleveland and did pretty well, and then came back as a starter the next year."

Same Division, New Team

In the seven seasons that Bill Brooks played for one of Buffalo's division rivals, the Indianapolis Colts, he had 41 receptions for 573 yards, a 14-yards-per-catch average, against the Bills. Buffalo won nine of those 14 games, including six of the last seven. So when the NFL free agency began in 1993, for the wide receiver, it was an "if you can't beat 'em, join 'em" situation, and he became a member of the three-time defending AFC champions.

"The Colts wanted me to come back, but wanted to work out a new salary structure and things of that nature," said Brooks, who came to Buffalo with 411 career catches and 28 touchdowns.

"If I'm not mistaken, back then, the Bills, since they had gone to the Super Bowl, couldn't approach anyone unless they lost someone. So after they lost someone, they talked to me and my agent, worked out a deal, and I signed. [Colts owner] Jim Irsay understood everything that was going on, and he wished me the best and wished things could have worked out [so that] I stayed with the Colts. He's always been a great owner and a great friend to me.

"It was a little different at first after you go up there and you have a different uniform on. The players, the organization, the fans in Buffalo welcomed me with open arms, and that was great. They were great to me."

With 60 receptions and five touchdowns during his first season with the Bills, Brooks finished second on the team to tight end Pete Metzelaars's 68 grabs and helped post a 12–4 record and win the division. In the first playoff game against the Raiders, he led Buffalo with six catches for 96 yards and two touchdowns.

"I don't know if I was in the zone or not, but I just knew that Jim [Kelly] was throwing me the ball and I was just trying to do my best to catch it," Brooks laughed. "It was a fairly cold day out there. The field was quite slippery, so my thing was to just make sure I kept my balance and, if the ball came my way, to concentrate because it was moving a little bit in the wind. That was it; I just caught the ball. In the zone or not? I don't know. I just think my number was called more than anything else."

Paup Star

Sure, they didn't bring home a Lombardi Trophy from the four trips to the Super Bowl, but the Bills did notch a win during the 1995 NFL free-agency period when they signed Bryce Paup.

After playing for five seasons in Green Bay, a team that had gone to the previous two playoffs as an NFC Wild Card team, the linebacker's last game wearing a Packers helmet was in the 1994 Pro Bowl.

"They [the Bills] had what I thought was still a great nucleus that had made four Super Bowl runs," Paup said. "The offense was still together, and they were trying to improve their defense and had just signed [linemen] Ted Washington and Jim Jeffcoat. They still had Bruce Smith and Cornelius Bennett and the rest of the group, so I figured with the style of defense they played and how they treated the players and everything that that would be a good fit for me."

Initially, though, the fit was not so comfortable. Paup was replacing 12-year veteran and team leader Darryl Talley, who had been released by Buffalo. "When I got to the first minicamp, Bruce Smith and Cornelius Bennett were wearing Talley's number. That kind of made me a little apprehensive. I don't know, I guess there was a feeling of maybe intrusion. Like they wished they would have kept Talley because he was a good player and had been there forever, and he was a friend. They'd been in a bunch of battles with him, so I can understand that. But after that, for the most part, the team definitely received me well. I was treated fine. Those things eventually wear out, and you move on with life. That's just the fact of the NFL now—people move on."

During that first season, Paup moved to among the top echelon of the league's linebackers. On September 17 the Bills hosted Indianapolis in the third game of the season and won, 20–14. Paup sacked Colts quarterback Jim Harbaugh three times, had 14 tackles, and forced two fumbles, earning the AFC Defensive Player of the Week award for the first of two times. He was later selected as November's AFC Player of the Month. And with a career-high and league-leading 17.5 sacks to go along with 126 tackles, he was named the NFL's Defensive Player of the Year.

"We were playing the Jets in New York [on November 19, a 28–26 victory], and Bruce Smith said something to me at the end of the game: 'I'll help you become Defensive Player of the Year.' Until he said that, that never even crossed my mind," said Paup. "I was just hoping to make it back to the Pro Bowl. Those kinds of awards were, to me, saved for a Bruce Smith, Cornelius Bennett,

Rod Woodson, Deion Sanders, Reggie White, people like that. I just remember being kind of baffled by that statement because I'd never seen myself in that light before. It was just something totally unexpected."

A Modern-Day Throwback

Let's face it. There are times when a team just has good luck dropped on its doorstep. For each of the eight seasons that he played in the NFL, Chris Spielman led the Detroit Lions in tackles, and he was selected to play in the Pro Bowl four times. But then the linebacker seemed to fall out of favor with the organization because of his salary, and he became a free agent.

"In the first quarter of the [1995] season opener, against the big running back by the name of Bam Morris, I partially tore a pectoral muscle. I played through it and still had a good year," Spielman said. "I was coming up to be a free agent, and I think I wanted a little bit too much money. They didn't have it. They wanted to put it into an offensive guy. They really didn't pursue me, so I pursued free agency, and Buffalo was one of the teams that I was attracted to. They liked me, and they lost Cornelius Bennett to the Falcons that year, so that opened up room for me. That's why I ended up in Buffalo."

As was the case in Detroit, Spielman became an unquestioned team leader with the Bills about the same time he shut his car door after first arriving at the stadium in Orchard Park in 1996.

"I think if you're a veteran and you produce, you assume a role," said Spielman, who averaged 142 tackles per season with the Lions. "I think my position that I played was a leadership role automatically by the nature of the position, at least on the field. I started calling plays, and once I was familiar with the defense and what we were trying to do, I wasn't afraid to assert myself. When the coaches tell you what's expected of you, and you're there to do the job, you pretty much do it. I had credibility with the players because I was a player for a few years and was able to produce.

So most guys figured, 'Well, he's the linebacker, he's calling the plays, everybody line up and here we go.'"

Beginning with the season opener against the New York Giants when he totaled 17 tackles and recovered a fumble during overtime that set up the game-winning field goal, Spielman led the Bills in stops in 13 games and accumulated a career-high and team-record 206 tackles. However, statistics, as far as Spielman is concerned, are just clutter in a media guide. His mind-set when taking the field was very clear.

"Win! Pure and simple, win! It was all about winning. I didn't care when it was or where it was, as long as we did everything we could do to win the game. That was the mind-set. And winning's hard in the NFL. It's difficult. It didn't always happen, but you always did everything in the world in your own power to make it happen."

chapter 4

...and Going

Less than three years after he rushed for his record 2,003 yards, O.J. Simpson asked the Bills to trade him to a team that was closer to his home in Los Angeles.

A Delayed Trade

Offense. Defense. Special teams. The three phases of football. Buffalo's offensive lineman George Flint could have made an argument during the 1965 season that trades be added to the list.

"In the middle of the season, I was traded to Oakland, [but] the trade was not to be made until the season was over with," said Flint. "What happened was, we played the Kansas City Chiefs at the trade deadline. We needed a wide receiver. Glenn Bass and Elbert Dubenion were both knocked out for the season. We needed a deep threat. So they made the deal to pick up Bo Roberson, who came the next week. They [the Raiders] had their choice of a ballplayer after we froze so many [on the roster], and they chose [second-year defensive tackle] Tom Keating. Well, in that Kansas City game, Tom got a knee injury and was out for the season, so Oakland had the choice of another ballplayer, and I was the ballplayer they chose."

Following Buffalo's second straight AFL championship, both Flint and Keating ended up going to Oakland to complete the deal.

"I wasn't happy," laughed Keating. "In fact, I didn't even know. Buffalo never told me they traded me. It was after Christmas and I was back home in Chicago visiting my parents. There was nobody at the Bills office, so I called the Raiders and asked for Al Davis. 'Hey, it's winter here, and I have to buy some tires for my car.' He said to me, 'I don't think you're going to need any snow tires, young man.'

"I thought, 'Jeez, where am I going?' They had one good year and then they had been a struggling team. But I got out there and I really liked it. It was made for me, or I was made for it. Just perfect."

The First Free Agent

Not only was Pete Gogolak the first soccer-style kicker in professional football, but in 1966 he also became the first free agent to

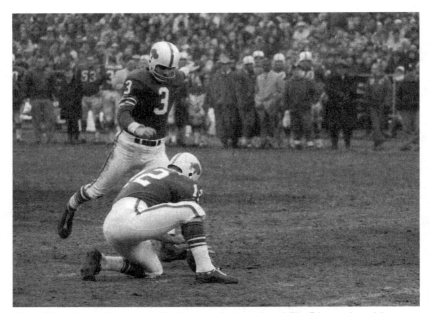

Pete Gogolak attempts a field goal during the AFL Championship Game against the San Diego Chargers on December 26, 1964, in Buffalo, New York.

jump from the AFL to the rival NFL, when he signed with the New York Giants.

"When I signed with the Bills [in 1964], I signed a one-year contract and a one-year option; that means I'm obligated to play for the Bills for two years," said Gogolak. "Being the second-highest scorer in the league [behind Boston's Gino Cappelletti] as a rookie, I asked for a raise, and they wouldn't give it to me. I'll tell you very frankly, I signed for $11,000, and I asked for $20,000. So I played out my contract and became a free agent. I didn't talk to anybody, and [when the contract expired on May 1, 1966] that's when the Giants approached me and signed me."

Suffice it to say, Bills fans did not hold a tickertape parade for Gogolak in front of Buffalo's City Hall.

"I think they thought I was a traitor, basically," laughed Gogolak. "I really loved Buffalo and I loved the team. It was a great football town. Very frankly, it was the best two years in my professional career, and it was a wonderful place to play for. The whole town was behind you. I think it was just kind of a financial situation. I felt that I was worth that kind of money, and management felt that I wasn't.

"I was the first player to switch leagues, and that created a lot of emotion. Actually, I was hoping somebody from the AFL was going to call me. You could read it any way you wanted to read it, but being the second-highest scorer in the league and nobody from the AFL calls and says, 'Hey, listen. We need a kicker,' it's kind of surprising. Then the Giants called and basically gave me a nice contract. So I jumped leagues, and basically the shit hit the fan. [Then–AFL commissioner] Al Davis started calling the NFL players, and some of the NFL owners called the AFL players, and basically what happened was six months later, the two leagues merged."

Lamonica's Sent West

Approaching the 1967 season, after four seasons as Buffalo's backup quarterback, Daryle Lamonica thought that he'd be seeing more playing time and that he just may, in the immediate future, be taking the field with the starters. But on March 14, just two and a half months after capturing their second straight AFL title and the day of the AFL and NFL's inaugural combined college draft, the Bills traded him along with wide receiver Glenn Bass and third- and fifth-round draft picks to Oakland for quarterback Tom Flores, wide receiver Art Powell, and a second-round draft selection that year.

"I was shocked! The night before I had talked to Ralph Wilson Jr. and Sr., and they both told me they were looking forward to me being their starting quarterback," said Lamonica. "Hell, I was all jazzed up! I could have run through brick walls! Eight hours later, I was traded. It's how I found out about the trade, I guess, that was the biggest shock to me and disappointing from my standpoint.

"I was in Fresno, California, and some buddies came up and said, 'Hey, you've been traded to the Raiders.' I said, 'Yeah, yeah, yeah, okay.' I had to call the *Fresno Bee*, my hometown paper, to find out. Well, I was devastated from having talked to the Bills organization the night before. And to this day, I have never heard from the Bills in regards to the trade or why I was traded."

Lamonica's attention quickly focused on the AFL's upcoming schedule and Oakland's game in War Memorial Stadium on October 15. "I started training right then and there for that particular game," Lamonica said.

He and Kemp each completed two touchdown passes but also combined for six interceptions. The Raiders won the game, 24–20, their first victory in Buffalo since 1961. "I thought I would play more [while with the Bills], but as I found out, it's a business. As it worked out, it was the best thing that could have happened for me. It gave me an opportunity to come back to the West Coast, where I was born and raised. My family could come up and see the games."

Good-bye, Dancing Bear

After eight seasons with the Bills, Ron McDole—a team captain, a two-time AFL All-Star, and a starting defensive end on the 1964 and 1965 AFL championship teams—had every right to feel secure on the team.

But on May 11, 1971, following two seasons under head coach John Rauch, McDole was traded to the Washington Redskins. As it turned out, it was a move that would result in both the player and the coach packing up and leaving Buffalo.

"John was kind of paranoid. He thought everybody was against him, I guess. He would change our defense, and we had a great defense. Even though we were losing, we were in the top couple defenses in the league," said McDole. "We tried to play his defense. We just didn't have the personnel. So we struggled with that, we struggled with him, and we struggled and struggled and struggled all year long.

"I was one of the captains, and I remember saying to [defensive tackle] Jim Dunaway, 'Let's bury the axe [with Rauch] and see what we can do.' So I went and talked to him in the off-season. We sat around, and I explained to him that we were going to do everything we could do. And about three weeks later I was traded. I was kind of surprised in that standpoint.

"He [Rauch] went on a television show and said something to do with [that] I didn't play up to my potential. I was kind of amused. I led the team in tackles that year. I didn't have that bad of a year. Apparently he just tried to make an excuse why I was traded. And eventually, I guess what happened, the people in Buffalo put so much pressure on the organization that Ralph Wilson—and of course, Ralph told me this—he said, 'I had to make a statement.' He came out publicly and said that I was not a bad player. It [the trade] was not on account of my play. Rauch said that if he [Wilson] did that, he would resign. Of course, Wilson probably jumped up and down over that. It got him out of the contract.

"It didn't make any difference to me at that time. I was gone, and it was the greatest thing that ever happened to me. I was able to play eight more years. If I stayed there it would have been the end of my career."

Juice Wants Out

Prior to the 1976 training camp, less than three years after bringing the focus of football fans everywhere upon Buffalo by rushing for an NFL record 2,003 yards, O.J. Simpson asked the Bills to trade him to a California-based team that was closer to his home in Los Angeles.

Simpson had rushed for 1,817 yards in 1975, the second-highest total of his seven-year career; had 426 receiving yards, his highest total; and found the end zone a league-record 23 times. In short, as far as the Bills were concerned, if they decided to grant his request, it was definitely a seller's market.

Buffalo's owner, Ralph Wilson, reportedly wanted three quality veterans in return for the star running back. He didn't get them even though he had had extended talks with the Rams. An unhappy Simpson decided to hold out.

"I was trying to be traded only because the Bills had traded away all their players, and there was no way that they were going to be competitive," said Simpson. "I knew my time was running out, and if I was going to have a chance to play on a championship team, I had to leave Buffalo. If Buffalo was going to be a championship team, they had to get more players. Obviously, the smart thing at that time would have been to make a deal with the Rams for me. Evidently, their negotiations broke down."

One day before the Bills opened the season against Miami on *Monday Night Football*, Simpson and Wilson had their own negotiations conclude when they agreed on a reported three-year, $2.5 million contract. The owner would later say that he learned his negotiating lesson from the running back.

"Our situation was unusual at the time, and it turned out to be to my advantage," Simpson said. "I'll never feel that I was ever overpaid in Buffalo. If I got overpaid at the end, it was just catching up from some other times of my career. Ralph and I had our problems in negotiations with my feelings about being traded to L.A., but at no time did Ralph and I stop speaking or were we upset with one another. Ralph is a standup guy!"

Shipped Across the Lake

One of the finest offensive linemen to ever play the game, Bills guard Joe DeLamielleure finished five consecutive seasons [1975–79] by playing in the Pro Bowl. He credits his success in Buffalo to his position coach and later head coach, Jim Ringo, and his blue-collar work ethic.

"Jim Ringo was tremendous," said DeLamielleure. "The guy was a technician. The world could blow up and Jim would only want to know if you're going to block the guy over you. He was beyond focused. He taped his ankles for the first game he coached. He let us play, but he also made us do it the right way. We did it over and over and over. You could do it in your sleep! He was the perfect coach for me.

"Secondly, I had a lot of ability when I was playing, but I worked like I had none. Guys would say, 'You come to camp like you're trying to make the team every year.' I actually came in early with the rookies a couple times. I just enjoyed it. I liked working hard, and I liked doing the little things that would make you good. I loved football. I loved playing it. I loved being in Buffalo."

Well, he did love being in Buffalo. DeLamielleure's admiration diminished after Chuck Knox replaced Ringo as the team's head coach in January 1978. And after asking to be traded and holding out during the 1980 training camp, he was headed to Cleveland after a deal was made a week before the regular season opened.

"Maybe I was immature at the time, but I felt that I did everything I could do as a player and they brought in a couple guys, one was a guy named [Isiah] Butch Robertson. I was just wondering about them," DeLamielleure said. "Then they let [Jim] Braxton go and they traded Bobby Chandler, and I said, 'Wait a second! I worked my butt off. I'm a five-time All-Pro and they bring in a guy who is a little bit questionable with his character? And he's getting paid a whole lot more than me?' I never once complained that I want to be the highest-paid guy or any of that stuff, but he was making *a whole lot more than me*! And I said, 'This is crazy!'

"I'm always for the underdog and doing the right thing, and I didn't think they were doing the right thing at that time, so I wanted to take a stand. It had a little bit to do with money, but it also had more to do with character. I felt that I busted my butt for Buffalo, and I thought they should come to me and say, 'Hey! You should be one of the highest-paid guys on the team. Not some guy getting double what you're getting.' That kind of ticked me off. One thing grew into another. Chuck and I didn't get along. Probably it was my fault. I'll take the blame on that. I should have kept my mouth shut. I remember Paul Maguire said, 'Keep your mouth shut. You'll be in the Hall of Fame if you be quiet. Stay here and you'll go to 10 Pro

Bowls.' At the time I thought, screw this! I want to do the right thing. But that was my biggest regret. That I ever left Buffalo."

Trading the Number One

Tom Cousineau, Buffalo's and the league's number one draft pick in 1979, never found his way to the team's training camp at Niagara University. He instead headed north of the border to play for the CFL's Montreal Alouettes. But in March 1982, he bid au revoir to his Canadian team and returned home with the intention of playing in the NFL.

The Bills had retained the rights to the former Ohio State All-America linebacker during his CFL tenure and could have him on their roster by matching any contract offer an NFL team rendered him. And there were rumors that Buffalo planned to do just that. The Houston Oilers tested that speculation and signed him to a reported five-year, $3.5 million offer sheet, which included a $1 million signing bonus.

The Bills matched it, only to then trade Cousineau to his home-town Cleveland Browns for their first-round draft choice in 1983, their third-round selection in 1984, and their fifth-round selection in 1985.

"The three years I was in Montreal, the company line out of the Buffalo front office was that if I was going to play in the NFL, I was going to wear a Buffalo uniform," said Cousineau. "We did our thing. We talked to a number of teams. We came out with what we feel is an excellent offer from the Houston Oilers. We signed a deal, the offer sheet was sent to the Bills, and then all of a sudden their stand wavers a bit. They don't respond. At that point, I was pretty certain that something was going to happen. They were going to try to make a trade. The offer sheet was very simple. It was one page with about six lines, and they said that they had to analyze it. Well, I had given them more credit business-wise. To analyze something that was not very complex at all, I felt that they were looking for a way out of the situation, which they were.

"I didn't speak to anybody from Buffalo. They never once called me during the time I was negotiating with other teams. What they wanted to do, basically, they said that they were going to match any offer that came down the pike, or across the table. I think they did that to scare people off, to intimidate them into not making an offer. Because what's the use? Buffalo's going to hit it anyway. Well, that wasn't the case. I think that it got a little out of hand. They needed to talk with both myself and [my agent] Jimmy Walsh to come to terms. They couldn't have made the deal themselves, and I think that's where they made the mistake, with not talking to us and not trying to work things out."

Backtracking the three years to when he was initially drafted, did Cousineau even want things to be worked out so he could play for the Bills?

"I was very proud to be Buffalo's number one pick in '79," he said. "They let me know well in advance that they were going to draft me, and did I have any problems with that? I replied, 'No,' and that was the truth. The problem came when they offered me a very embarrassing contract. What made even less sense was when they didn't sign me, they turned around and hired a man named Isiah Robertson. I don't understand that! I think that my position was very well justified. It was pointed out even further with the Robertson deal."

Sweet Home Alabama

Not Cookie, not O.J., no player rushed for more yards during his first season with the Bills than Joe Cribbs did in 1980. Finishing second to Houston's Earl Campbell in the AFC with 1,185 yards, the second-round draft pick out of Auburn was named the conference's Rookie of the Year and selected to start in the Pro Bowl.

Proving that he was not a "one-year wonder," Cribbs led Buffalo in rushing the following three seasons and was the team's top receiver in 1983 as well. However, three weeks before he was scheduled to report for the 1984 training camp, unhappy with his contract, the three-time Pro Bowl selection signed a personal-services deal with the USFL's Birmingham Stallions. The Bills were unsuccessful with legal maneuvering to keep him in Buffalo, and he jumped leagues, returning to his home state of Alabama.

"If you truly understand the game and statistics, I was playing on a team where, basically, I was probably 60 to 70 percent of our offense at that time," said Cribbs. "I had guys who were backing me up that were making more than I was making. That was just total injustice. But the thing that I feel that I would have done differently is, I would have at least kept my doors open as opposed to just saying, 'Hey, okay, they don't want me. I'm leaving.' Then when they came back, I said, 'Nah, it's too late.' I would have done that differently.

"I don't regret it. You have to make sure that you understand what I'm saying...I probably would have been more inclined to continue to discuss things out with Buffalo before I actually left to go to the USFL. I would have been a little bit more open. I think back then, and it's been a lot of water under the bridge now, but back then, my perception was that there was so much unwillingness on the part of the team at the time to even consider redoing my contract or taking a look at my contract.

"I don't think that anybody that's really being honest would say, if they could go back and do anything over, they would do it exactly as they did it. That's a scenario that you never get. Well, at least, that's an opportunity that you'll never get. I've heard a lot of people say, 'If I could do this over, I wouldn't change a thing.' And I know they're lying. Because I think everybody would. And sure, I would, too."

An Offer He Couldn't Refuse

The final three of the seven seasons that Will Wolford was with the Bills, they won 37 of 48 regular-season games, earned three AFC championships, and of course, played in three Super Bowls. He would conclude two of those campaigns in the Pro

Bowl. The left offensive tackle, like the team, took the field with a lot of confidence.

"It was a great feeling to play a home game those last couple years," said Wolford. "We knew we were going to win, the team we were playing knew we were going to win, and we all knew that afterwards we were going to Jim Kelly's house for a party. To have that kind of control and that kind of confidence, it was a lot of fun. It's the greatest city in the world to play in if you're winning. I've got friends who've played in the NFL who've hardly been on any winning teams much less played in the Super Bowl every year. So I was very fortunate to be a part of all that."

A 1986 first-round draft choice out of Vanderbilt, Wolford was not a part of Buffalo's fourth straight trip to the Super Bowl. After becoming a free agent following the 1992 season, the Bills made him one of their transition players, which meant that they had the right to match any offer he received from another team. Indianapolis tested to see if Buffalo was serious about that by reportedly offering Wolford a three-year, $7.65 million contract that included escalator clauses. The Bills argued that those clauses were unfair and filed a complaint with the NFL's management council. Buffalo lost the ruling and Wolford.

"It was [an offer] I certainly couldn't refuse. Not only were they making me the highest-paid lineman in the league, they were making me the highest-paid lineman in the league times two! And they were putting in playing-time clauses that would guarantee me to be the highest-paid player on the team. It was hardly an offer that I could turn down," Wolford said. "It was a great contract and all that, but I was extremely sad to leave Buffalo. I was there year-round for seven years, so it was very difficult to walk. But looking at it, being an offensive lineman and having that kind of contract thrown in front of me, I had to sign it."

Wolford returned to Rich Stadium with a horseshoe on his helmet for the first time on November 21, 1993, with mixed emotions.

"I was playing against friends for the first time in my entire career. I mean, you grow up playing football, you hardly ever play against somebody you know. If you do know them, you usually don't like them," Wolford laughed. "And here I was playing against an entire team and playing in a city that I loved. It was very difficult, but the fans were really great."

When Super Bowl XXVIII rolled around, Wolford was just like most of those fans and watched the Bills meet the Dallas Cowboys on television. "I was in the Caribbean and actually just sat in a hotel room and watched it with about a case of beer. It was a weird feeling to watch all my buddies play in that Super Bowl," he said. "Having played in the previous three and having my opportunity as a player, I was really hoping and I really thought they would have their best chance to win that game. I knew all the distractions we had in the previous Super Bowls. I thought that hopefully that would not happen again. A football is shaped funny and a lot of funny things happen on a field because of it. I was just hoping the bounces would go their way."

"Was It a Mistake? Sure."

Shane Conlan, the third linebacker ever chosen in the first round by the Bills, did not waste any time proving he was worthy of being selected so high in 1987. Starting off on the outside, he stepped into the middle, an unfamiliar position, after Buffalo acquired Cornelius Bennett in a trade, and led the team with 114 tackles, earning the Associated Press's NFL Defensive Rookie of the Year award.

Beginning with his second season, in 1988, Conlan was named to three consecutive Pro Bowls. "I was a pretty confident player," he said. "I think I'm a pretty good judge of talent. I can pretty much call when a guy's a good player. And at that time, that was before Junior Seau came in and, I don't know, I thought I was one of the better ones [linebackers], to tell you the truth. It was obviously a very big honor."

Following the 1992 campaign and Buffalo's third straight trip to the Super Bowl, Conlan received a very big contract offer. From the Rams! St. Louis offered the unrestricted free agent a three-year deal that was reportedly worth $5.6 million. Conlan accepted it and headed west after six seasons with the Bills.

"Was it a mistake? Sure. I probably should have stayed. But financially, you just can't turn down that kind of money. Right after, when I signed, Marv [Levy] called me and said, 'Yeah, we want you, but it's just too high.' I understood. Any idiot would say, 'Listen, you're going from a team that just went to a Super Bowl to a team that...' But at the time, the year before, the Rams were .500 [actually 6–10]. That was [head coach] Chuck Knox's second year, and I was thinking these guys can win. But then they fired Chuck and brought in Rich Brooks. And then they fired him and brought in [Dick] Vermeil. I was there three years, and we won a total of eight games, maybe nine [actually 16]. It was bad."

While the grass was not greener in St. Louis, Conlan remained the same hardworking, stick-his-nose-in-the-middle-of-the-action linebacker the final three years of his career that he was during the first six. "When I came up [from Penn State], I was fast, and I think I could hit big people well. That's one thing I did throughout my career. I could always hit the bigger people, get off of them, and make plays. [If I] had to do it over again, I'd have gone around them and I'd still be playing, maybe," Conlan laughed. "But that's one thing I found I was pretty good at."

Role Player Rolled Out the Door

For six seasons, Bills running back Kenneth Davis was as reliable as duct tape. A backup to Thurman Thomas, he would have likely been a starter on many other NFL clubs. Yet he was happy with his role and was a sound contributor to the team's four consecutive AFC championship titles.

And while he had many fine moments on the field during the regular seasons, Davis seemingly glowed during the playoffs: scoring three touchdowns against the Raiders in the 1990 AFC Championship Game; totaling 319 rushing yards during the four-game 1992 postseason; starting in Super Bowl XXVI when Thomas was temporarily helmetless; and leading the Bills in rushing in the following two Super Bowls. But during the 1995 off-season, Davis was reminded that professional football was not just about *X*s and *O*s; it was at times a somewhat brutal business.

"I think one of the hardest things in my life was when the Bills told me they didn't want me back. I felt I wasn't through playing," said Davis, who originally signed with Buffalo as a Plan B free agent in 1989. "It was a decision that they made that they didn't need me back or want me back or whatever. I went in to talk about the situation. What were we going to do about the season coming up? Were we going to start working on my contract now or later? John Butler said, 'We're not going to re-sign you.'

"When I left, John Butler pretty much knew that I really didn't want to go play anywhere else. Maybe it was selfish or stupidity on my behalf, but that's just how much I cared about the organization and playing under Coach Levy. I could have gone to a couple other teams; the Carolina Panthers offered me a contract. I didn't take it. I just felt confined to Buffalo. It was where I wanted to be, where I had been. I didn't want to be a player that just bounced all around the league. So I just got out. It was time to accept that and move on. Buffalo is a very special city to me. And it was a very special team."

chapter 5

Patrolling the Sideline

Buffalo Bills coach Lou Saban, left, lets out a cheer with three of his top players—Pete Gogolak (3), Jack Kemp (15), and Wray Carlton (30)—after winning the 1964 American Football League championship. The Bills defeated the San Diego Chargers 20–7. (Photo courtesy of AP/Wide World Photos)

Saban Goes to Work

Lou Saban is synonymous with Bills firsts. He was on the sideline when the team earned its first victory on September 23, 1960, in Boston. He was, however, the head coach of the Patriots at the time. He joined Buffalo as the director of player personnel on October 27, 1961, and replaced Buster Ramsey as the head coach less than three months later. He was instrumental in turning the team around, guiding it to its first winning season in 1962.

"I've always felt that you've got to be a good trader, be able to understand the market. I think we did," said Saban. "I had a very good coaching staff. Almost every one of them became head coaches. We could understand talent. Taking it from [my former coach] Paul Brown, I kept saying, 'You win with talent, and you have to make sure you coach them properly.' That was what we were able to do. I didn't want the players to lean on the coaches. I wanted them to feel the coaches were leaning on them. When they're out on that football field and they're in trouble, they've got to help themselves. The men I coached were an experienced group. You're talking about Tom Sestak, Billy Shaw, Cookie Gilchrist, Jack Kemp, Daryle Lamonica, right down the line. As a group, they were tough to beat. They were my pride and joy."

Saban's "tough to beat" group was indeed tough to beat. In 1964 the Bills recorded a 12–2 record and won the AFL championship. In 1965 they were 10–3–1 and won the league title again. Yet, surprisingly, he resigned a week after that second championship-game victory over San Diego.

"In a person's own life, there are certain adjustments you think you have to make," said Saban, a two-time AFL Coach of the Year. "At that stage, because of my family, I thought maybe this might be a chance to make one of those adjustments. I tried to see if I could put a very difficult atmosphere, tied in with what I thought was a very congenial situation at home, and keep pressure off my family. That was impossible to do. Youngsters who happen to be children of head coaches in professional sports don't have it easy. I just couldn't fathom how difficult it was to make changes in that type of an atmosphere. But I gave it a try."

Knox Landing

Chuck Knox's reputation for success preceded him. Hired for his first head-coaching job by the Rams in 1973, he guided Los Angeles to the penthouse of the NFC West division. And so with the goal to move into the AFC East's top floor, in 1978 the hardworking Knox was hired by the Bills as their vice president in charge of football operations. In other words, he was the new head coach.

"Ralph Wilson came out and visited with me and told me what he wanted to do," explained Knox. "I'd just finished five years within which we won five straight divisional championships. Fifty-four wins, 15 losses, one tie. And that was playing a 14-game schedule. So the Bills job appealed to me because they had won like three or four games [actually five] over a two-year period, and I felt like we could go in there and turn the program around."

Knox's willingness to tackle such an adventuresome project, considering that the Bills had only played in a single playoff game since the leagues merged in 1970, no doubt shocked at least a few around the league. "Anytime you leave a team like the L.A. Rams," said Knox, "where we were winning big, and going to situations like that, where they were having a lot of problems, I think it surprised a lot of people.

"The goal always is to win the Super Bowl championship. But in light of that, you've got to put a competitive team out on the field, which they obviously didn't have those last couple of years before we got there. We had to change the attitude of the team. We had to completely redo the scouting department, which wasn't much of anything. So we hired some scouts. We brought Norm Pollom in [as the director of college scouting], who had been with me with the Rams. And then we also went and got some veteran players to bring some toughness. We became a pretty good football team. We were competitive that first year."

"When Chuck took over it was like a breath of fresh air," said third-year defensive end Ben Williams. "We hadn't been very successful. What Chuck did when he came was he brought the team together and showed us a lot of unity and how to win. Nobody ever taught you how to win early in my career."

A Marvelous Hire

When a team loses 13 of 15 games dating back to the previous season, a coaching change is not surprising. Dropping seven of their first nine games in 1986, the Bills replaced Hank Bullough with Marv Levy, who was the director of football operations for the CFL's Montreal Alouettes. Levy arrived in Buffalo to take over the struggling team with an open and curious mind.

"I knew the names of the players in the room, but I couldn't have pointed out Jim Kelly or Bruce Smith or any of those guys," laughed Levy. "I know what I said initially: 'What it takes to win is simple, but it isn't easy. Run, throw, block, tackle, catch, and kick better than your opponent. We're not going to do it with a bunch of Xs and Os. We're not going to do it with a bunch of talk. We're going to go to work on fundamentals.' And I did point out to them, 'I'm going to ask three questions for you to answer. I know mine. Where are we now? Where do we want to go? How are we going to get there?'"

Three of the team leaders who were at the meeting and would have to help Levy and the Bills "get there" were Kelly, Smith, and Darryl Talley.

"You always hope, you always pray that that's going to be the case, but you really don't know," said Kelly. "You just go with what you've heard about the man. You just hope that the owner, Ralph Wilson, gets the right players behind you, and then it's up to you to do your job. The coaches can only do so much coaching. When you get on the field, it's up to the players to make the plays."

"We felt that it was the beginning of something special," Smith said. "We knew his personality was contagious and that he had a

Marv Levy made Bills history by winning his first game as the new coach in 1986. He pulled the team out of an incredible slump with his unique coaching methods. (Photo courtesy of AP/Wide World Photos)

great deal of integrity. And if any of that rubbed off on us, we felt that we were headed in the right direction."

Added Talley, "I didn't know what really to expect. I just sat there and watched and just sort of looked at what he was doing. I was trying to figure out exactly which way I was going and what we were going to do as a team. How was he going to treat us, and how were we going to react?"

Levy would make team history during his first week on the job by becoming the first head coach to win his first game, topping Pittsburgh, 16–12. "I didn't know that," said Levy, who was Kansas City's head coach from 1977 to 1982. "I'm surprised because there have been some good ones. Lou Saban and Chuck Knox, to name a couple. I'm pleased to know that we won any games. That it happened to be the first one, great!"

Kelly agreed that the timing could not have been better, and beating the Steelers—that was a personal bonus. "It might make me a little different than anybody else because I grew up in Pittsburgh, and I wanted to play for the Steelers, and here I am playing against the team that I grew up watching and cheering for. The Terrible Towel, Franco [Harris], [Terry] Bradshaw, [John] Stallworth, [Lynn] Swann, Mean Joe Greene, all those guys! So that was a memory from when I was a little kid, and here I'm playing against that team. It was exciting!

"We'd just come off of a heart-wrenching loss against Tampa Bay the week before, and here we've got a new coach and a new identity. I was looking forward to it. I was looking forward to the change. So for me, it was just a matter of waiting and seeing what happened. And it turned out being the best thing the Buffalo Bills ever did, hiring a guy like Marv Levy."

chapter 6

Touched by a Saban

Mike Stratton delivered the "hit heard 'round the world" to Chargers running back Keith Lincoln in the 1964 AFL Championship Game.

An In with the Boss

Booker Edgerson arrived in Buffalo as a rookie free-agent corner-back in 1962 with an advantage. His coach at Western Illinois University three years earlier was the same man who was the Bills' head coach at the time, Lou Saban.

"When he got the call to be the coach [of the AFL's Boston Patriots in 1960], Leroy Jackson, Larry Garron, and myself said, 'Don't forget us when we graduate,'" Edgerson said. "I was playing baseball and had signed a contract with the Patriots, but in those days you could not participate in college sports and sign a professional contract. I just told them to hold on to it until the baseball season was over with. But in the meantime he got fired. So he asked me what I wanted to do with the contract. I said just tear it up, throw it away, and wherever he ends up, give me a call."

In addition to calling players that he was familiar with such as Edgerson, the coach was handing out pink slips. A lot of pink slips! Prospective players did not really face a secure future during Buffalo's training camps under Saban.

"Saban got rid of a lot of folks between '62 and '64," laughed Edgerson. "A lot of guys were hollering and screaming. They didn't feel comfortable and they didn't feel this. And he said, 'Hey! I don't feel comfortable either. [But] I'm going to fire somebody before they fire me!' And basically, that's what it was.

"We'd go on a road trip, in particular in North Carolina [during the 1963 preseason], and they cut a guy basically on the bench and traded him to [that game's opponent] Denver. The guy wanted to get back on the plane and they told him, 'No, you'll have to get on the other team's plane.'

"And we had a situation in Houston where I think there had to be five or six guys that they cut right then! Cut them on the spot! It was brutal, but I guess it was something he had to do. It goes back to the story that he said, 'I will fire somebody before I get fired.' The [remaining] guys took it really seriously and worked very hard to maintain some kind of consistency in their play, and it all paid off."

Dial *84 for Warlick

During the foundation-building days of the American Football League, the eight teams recruited players by scouting games and practices, watching game films or, in the case of tight end Ernie Warlick, over the telephone.

"I received a call from a guy just out of the blue asking me how I was doing and did I ever plan to move to the AFL or NFL, come back to the States? I said, 'I don't know, maybe in the future.' I had no idea who this guy was. But as it turned out, apparently he was somebody that knew [recently hired Bills head coach Lou] Saban," said the three-time Canadian Football League All-Star.

Buffalo was not the only team in the league that was aware of Warlick. He was also contacted by the Boston Patriots and the New York Titans. "Well, the Titans, I went there and I just didn't like what I saw. Harry Wismer was the owner at the time, and when he found out I was going to talk to another AFL team, he was going to sue," laughed Warlick. "I just didn't like the whole operation there. I was living in Washington, D.C., at the time, and Saban called me up and came to see me. He wanted to talk to me because he was coming to Buffalo and he'd like for me to come with him. So we went out to dinner, and I signed up that night to come to Buffalo."

During the 1962 campaign, Buffalo's leading quarterback Warren Rabb completed 67 passes. Warlick had 35 catches. The following season, Warlick was still a target with 24 receptions. They, however, came from a new quarterback, but someone he was still familiar with, Jack Kemp.

"Kemp and I were both in the Canadian League. We both went to training camp, I think, in '57 or '58. He and Tom Flores [who was with the Bills from 1967 to 1969] were released from up there, and I stayed. That type of offense up there requires a quarterback that could run the ball and neither one of these guys were great runners. So this was my second time running into Kemp. I knew a little bit about how he could throw a ball. I thought that [claiming him off waivers from San Diego] was an excellent move."

Find a Line

Buffalo drafted 34 players during the 1962 AFL draft, including linebacker Mike Stratton. Granted, not all of them reported, instead opting for the NFL or going a different way for other reasons. That said, it's little wonder that the coaches had difficulty remembering who was who or, for that matter, who played what position.

"Buster Ramsey had always been partial about everyone from Tennessee, so he was pretty instrumental in my being drafted. But when I got to camp, [Lou] Saban, who was the personnel director, had become the head coach by that time, and I wanted to be a tight end," said Stratton. "Lou had called out all the names of the players we had in camp and what time we were supposed to go out [onto the field], and he never did call my name. So afterward, I walked over to him and said, 'Coach, what group would you like me to go out with?' He looked at me and says, 'What was your name again?' I told him, and he said, 'Ah, just go out there with someone.'

"Anyway, they had already got Ernie Warlick from the Canadian League, and he was pretty well set as their tight end, so I didn't get much of an opportunity. They started me at defensive end, and I tried to play a little bit there. And then we got a bunch of linebackers hurt, thank goodness, and they changed me to linebacker. It was just a series of very fortunate events."

With a career-high six interceptions during his rookie season, Stratton and the Bills were fortunate that he still possessed the soft hands of a tight end. "I'd always pictured myself as a tight end," said Stratton, who would deliver "the hit heard 'round the world" on San Diego's running back Keith Lincoln two years later in the AFL Championship Game. "Most linebackers, I think, came to linebacker from tight end. We sort of all pictured ourselves as tight ends, although not very many other people did."

Switch Back to Where You Were

An All-America offensive tackle at Penn State, Stew Barber was switched to outside linebacker as a rookie with the Bills in 1961. He made the transition from blocking to tackling and showed that he could catch the ball as well. Collecting three interceptions, he found the end zone in Denver with one after picking off Broncos quarterback Frank Tripucka and motoring 21 yards for the score.

However, when Lou Saban succeeded Buster Ramsey as the head coach in 1962, one of the moves he made was returning Barber to the offensive line. "[Following the 1961 season] I'd gone on a six-month program in the military. I worked my butt off to get my weight down because I weighed about 240," said Barber. "I came out of the service at about 220 and went to training camp. Saban, on about the second or third day, came to me and said, 'We're going to make an offensive tackle out of you.'"

The svelte Barber's reaction? "So be it. I gained 20 pounds in about two weeks and got my butt beat by everybody, blocking guys that were 270, 280. By the end of training camp, I'd gained about 20, 25 more pounds and still had all the quickness that was necessary for pass-blocking and all the other stuff. I'm glad that it worked out."

An Ed of All Trades

The thought of playing professional football did not cross Ed Rutkowski's mind until a representative of the Bills visited the Notre Dame campus in South Bend, Indiana, following the 1963 AFL draft. Rutkowski was persuaded to join his college teammates, quarterback Daryle Lamonica and linebacker Ed Hoerster, who were both drafted by the team, at Buffalo's training camp.

"The three of us were very good friends, and we decided we'd just give it a shot and see what happened," said Rutkowski. "Well, I made the team, believe it or not, as a cornerback. I was on the kickoff team [as the] outside man, and we were playing a preseason game in North Carolina, I think it was against the Denver Broncos. The outside man's responsibility is to make sure that nobody ever gets outside of you, that you force everything inside.

"We kicked off, and I happened to let the guy get outside of me, and they had a substantial kickoff return. And as I was coming to the sideline I could see [head coach Lou] Saban running out, and as soon as he got to me, he said, 'Rutkowski, you've got a lot of potential, and I think you've got a great chance of making this team. But if you ever, ever let another guy get outside of you on a kickoff return, you're not going to be wearing a Buffalo Bills uniform!' I never let another guy get outside of me."

Rutkowski, who would eventually be moved to halfback, then to receiver, and then to quarterback for the Bills later in his career, did see action on defense as a rookie. Albeit briefly.

"I actually got into a game against the San Diego Chargers when Booker Edgerson injured himself. He got, not a concussion, but almost got knocked out," Rutkowski said. "So I went in, and the first guy I had to cover was [future Hall of Fame wide receiver] Lance Alworth. He caught a 15-yard out on me, and they pulled me out of the game so fast it made your head spin, and they put Booker back in."

Buying a Leader

Lou Saban not only proved himself to be a successful coach for the Bills, but two days before he opened Buffalo's 1963 training camp, he showed that he was also a smart shopper when he bought veteran linebacker Harry Jacobs from the Boston Patriots.

"It was a great reaction just to be coming to the Bills. It took me out of a situation in Boston where Nick Buoniconti came in and was given my job," said Jacobs. "At that point in time, he wasn't as good as I was. That was my opinion anyhow. That was really frustrating for me. But Nick Buoniconti became a great linebacker, so there's nothing to be said about that from that perspective. It's just from a standpoint that at that point in time, I was the guy starting and I should have been. So the move to the Bills had no problem anyway other than a very positive happening for my future. That's the way I looked at it."

Saban certainly knew what he was buying, since he was the coach of the Patriots for two of the seasons, 1960 and 1961, that Jacobs was starting for Boston. Did he tell the linebacker what he expected from him?

"He didn't specifically state it, but it was pretty evident in the posture of the whole team that I was to be the defensive leader and get out there and do the job as the middle linebacker. Call the signals. And that's what I did."

A Second Chance Pays Off

Buffalo's Offensive Most Valuable Player in 1961, Glenn Bass combined the '61 and '62 seasons for 82 catches for 1,320 yards and seven touchdowns. Yet the wide receiver was released by head coach Lou Saban after the Bills opened the 1963 campaign with back-to-back losses.

"At that point, some of us were obviously not meeting his goals or what he thought his goals were," said Bass, who then drove to his home in Wilson, North Carolina—a 16-hour car trip—and traced his route back to Buffalo the following day. "I just disagreed with his assessment. I drove back and went to his home and told him that I didn't feel like I'd been treated fairly and didn't agree with his decision and that I would be on the taxi squad and prove my worth. So I was a halfback on the taxi squad for a couple weeks, and then I was placed back on the roster."

That would prove to be a brilliant move. Securely back in Saban's good graces, Bass made his presence known during the first half of the 1964 season with 22 receptions for 408 yards and was on the receiving end of five of Buffalo's 13 touchdown passes, including a team record 94-yarder against Houston on October 11.

He added his name to another team record on November 8, when the Bills took on the New York Jets before an AFL record crowd of 60,300 at Shea Stadium. With eight receptions, Bass totaled 231 yards, a 28.9-yards-per-catch average, and scored on an 80-yard pass play from Daryle Lamonica, who was in for Jack Kemp, late in the second quarter. Buffalo won its ninth straight game, 20–7.

"About everything was clicking," Bass said modestly. "Sideline patterns, a corner pattern, we had a square-in pattern that seemed to work. It was just one of those days."

The NFL's Top Pick

Walt Patulski had a unique and, at times, strained relationship with head coach Lou Saban. Both coming and going.

The NFL's top draft choice in 1972, Patulski, a unanimous All-America defensive end at Notre Dame as a senior and the Lombardi Award winner as the nation's top lineman, came to Buffalo the same year that Saban was back for his second stint with the organization, having guided the Bills to back-to-back AFL titles in 1964 and 1965.

"It was interesting. Lou really was responsible for drafting me, and he was also responsible for peddling me," said Patulski. "He gave me a fair shake. I don't think his methods of operation were particularly effective with my temperament and demeanor. I think there was a little bit of conflict there. I had come from an environment with Ara Parseghian as a head coach that really left it in the hands of the defensive line coach, and he was like an overseer or a manager. Lou was more hands-on, working more directly with some of the players. It wasn't an effective strategy with me, so it was a little bit strained. He was clearly in a rebuilding program in what he was looking for. He was trying a lot of different things and had players coming in. A lot of veterans came in and were gone quickly. But he was fair."

It is also fair to say that Patulski did not enjoy the same level of gridiron success in Buffalo that he had experienced at Notre

Dame. He did, however, have exceptional performances at times. An example: during a 24–17 victory in Baltimore on November 25, 1973, Patulski was credited with three pass deflections, five unassisted tackles, and two assists, and he sacked Colts quarterback Marty Domres, earning the NFL Defensive Player of the Week honor.

But after four seasons with the Bills, he was traded to the St. Louis Cardinals for their second-round draft choice in 1976, which Buffalo would use to select offensive tackle Joe Devlin from the University of Iowa.

"I got a call," Patulski said. "It was April Fool's Day, and what was an omen, was the day before, Mike Kadish and I were playing Lou Saban and [assistant coach] Jim Ringo in pinochle, and we beat them soundly. I think Lou just got his revenge and traded me. I was disappointed, was very disappointed, because I had made a commitment to the area, and it felt like the Bills hadn't honored their commitment to me. They were certainly within their rights, but I was disappointed."

chapter 7

Memories of the AFL Championship Seasons

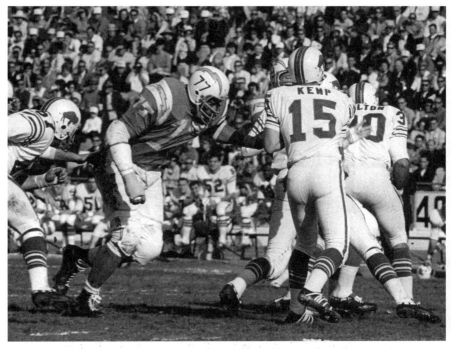

Defensive tackle Ernie Ladd of the San Diego Chargers pressures Bills quarterback Jack Kemp during the 1965 AFL Championship Game on December 26, 1965, at Balboa Stadium in San Diego. The Bills slaughtered the Chargers 23–0 to win their second consecutive AFL championship.

1964: 12–2: AFL Championship Game:

Buffalo 20, San Diego 7

1965: 10–3–1: AFL Championship Game:

Buffalo 23, San Diego 0

"We'd beaten them [San Diego] in Buffalo the first year and the second year we'd gone out there. The time frame we were in, *Sports Illustrated* didn't even recognize our [first] championship. That [the 1965 title game] was the first game they covered. They went out to San Diego and talked with the Chargers about the individuals they were going to play against. The magazine came out on the Thursday or Friday before we played that weekend, and to a man, just about, not very bright, these guys. They ended up talking about how they were going to kick everybody's butt! So we ended up with all kinds of motivation because of what we were reading, what they said they were going to do to us on the field come the game. That was a great, great effort by our team."

—Stew Barber, offensive tackle

"We were all concerned about each other. It was a good mixture of blue collar, white collar, black and white. It never was a race issue that I knew of. You hear a lot of coaches and players talk about being family, but it's hard to be family more than two or three years. The egos seem to get in the way. And then people start thinking about their own salary, etc. But it seemed to me in the '64 and '65 championship group, the chemistry was just good."

—Glenn Bass, wide receiver

"It was great. We were a family. We had a great time together. We all jelled. And then, of course, with everything else, through it all, you've got to have a lot of luck. A lot of luck."

—Al Bemiller, guard, center

"Well, let's see, number one, we were truly a great defensive team. Even though we had Cookie [Gilchrist] and Elbert Dubenion and Jack Kemp, I think anybody will tell you that the strength of the Buffalo Bills team was its defense during those years. It's very interesting because the two teams that we beat were both the San Diego Chargers. On paper, I didn't see how we could beat them. They had [Keith] Lincoln and [Paul] Lowe and [Lance] Alworth and [John] Hadl, [Dave] Kocourek, Ron Mix. And that was offense! Then they had Ernie Ladd and Earl Faison. I could almost repeat both sides of the ball verbatim because they were that good, that talented. So anyway, on paper, they looked to be very strong. But on game day, we were just very good, very confident. We just felt that our defense could play with anybody. I don't think we were favored in either one of the games, but we were just absolutely confident that we could beat the Chargers. And we did."

—Butch Byrd, cornerback

"We were more of a solid football team. We just didn't have any weaknesses. We weren't glamorous or anything. The key for us, and I'm sure all the guys would say that we were a ball-control offense. Just run the clock, get the first downs, get down there close enough that if you don't score a touchdown, kick a field goal and leave it up to our defense to give us the ball. We were a strong special teams. Paul Maguire was a great punter. We were just solid. We didn't have any spectacular players except Cookie. Most of our guys were just blue-collar guys that just went out and beat you. Just very methodical, mistake-free football. Ball-control, solid defense, great special teams, a good field-goal kicker with [Pete] Gogolak. We were just solid. There's nothing like winning."

—Wray Carlton, running back

"We had a great defense, and we had a heck of a running back, Cookie Gilchrist. And we had a real good offensive line. We controlled the ball; we would just move down the field. And then the defense would come in there and one, two, three, out! On one occasion, we told the defense, 'Don't get out so fast! We're tired!' They didn't allow anything. The defense was just great."

—Elbert Dubenion, wide receiver

"I think we played as a team and had some good talent to go with it. It just seemed that we worked together from '63 on and just seemed to jell. And I didn't think a coach was as important as they really are until [Lou] Saban left. When he left, Joe Collier was a fine defensive coordinator, a good man, and I liked him very much. But a difference in philosophy and the way you handle certain things in a ballgame, Saban just had a knack for that. I don't think we won but three or four games the next year after that year that Saban left."

—Jim Dunaway, defensive tackle

"We were extremely good on the defensive and offensive lines and just solid in every other position. Just solid! We didn't have a weakness. I played left guard [in the 1965 championship game after Billy Shaw was knocked out on the first play and sat out the rest of the half]. Actually Joe O'Donnell and I, both. We moved in and out of the game, so we played left and right guard. It's funny, I always felt like I could handle anybody. It was always a positive challenge for me because everybody was bigger than I was. As a matter of fact, at that stage of the game, the end of the season, I had intestinal flu, and I think I was down to 225. But it seems like I always played better injured or sick. Why that is, I don't know."

—George Flint, guard

"The key was, every time we ran on the field, we knew we were going to win. That type of a feeling. Plus Saban believed in a very cohesive veteran offensive line. We had a very good offensive line and also a pretty good defensive line. These guys—Billy Shaw and Al Bemiller and Ernie Warlick and Dave Costa, the tight ends— these guys were playing together and were kind of the heart of the team. And of course, Cookie Gilchrist was excellent. Every position, we had some strength and we just kind of blossomed. We just had a very good team, and we beat San Diego twice."

—Pete Gogolak, kicker

"I think that the defense was the best in the American Football League and we obviously felt we were the best in football at that point in time. The stable performance of our offense was just fantastic. The best defense is having the offense on the field. They did a great job for us. Jack [Kemp] was really a stable quarterback who did a great job. He was a super leader. So I would say it was a combination of both those things. The biggest part of it was that we had a great team that worked together and made things happen. We were supported tremendously by a great offense. We all played as a team. We didn't really care who got the credit for it just as long as we got the job done. And we got the job done. Everybody on the team was a hardworking type of personality who did their job."

—Harry Jacobs, linebacker

"In '64 we were successful because we had an all-around team. We had offense with Cookie and my passing. Good running and good blocking. And we had the greatest defense in the AFL with Tom Sestak and Butch Byrd and the guys. Saban was absolutely on fire. We went into Boston to play the Pats in a snowstorm, and we beat them [to clinch the Eastern Division title] and just jelled offensively and defensively. And I can't overestimate the contribution of Cookie Gilchrist, even though we had a flare-out when he got mad at me for throwing too many passes. But we really were good friends, and we are today, believe it or not. He just tore into the Pats at Fenway Park, and then we played the Chargers, and I think we felt we could beat anybody.

"The next year, Cookie was gone. We didn't quite have the offensive weapons, but we had a great defense. And we beat the heck out of the Chargers! They were so overconfident. I think they were two-touchdown favorites, and we whipped them convincingly. It was really, if not the capstone of my 10 years in the AFL, close to it."

—Jack Kemp, quarterback

"I had a lot of confidence in Lou Saban. I think he was an excellent coach. He treated everybody as men. We only had 36-man rosters then, and the chemistry was right with the guys. We played really well as a team. We worked hard, and the camaraderie we had as a team, it just jelled. We didn't care whether the offense won it, the defense won it, or special teams won it. We always seemed to pull it out. We were a physical team. We took a lot of pride in ourselves.

We played just as hard in the fourth quarter as we would in the first quarter. I think that made a difference. We just felt that we could win and nobody could beat us, and we played that way. Our chemistry was just perfect. Nobody dogged it. It didn't matter what the situation was or what the weather was; our defense could hit with the best of them. You knew you were going to be in a game because we fought for four quarters."

—Daryle Lamonica, quarterback

"The same thing that's the key today: no injuries. We had very few. In fact, when we went to the Chargers in '65, the only injury we had was Billy Shaw, who's now in the Hall of Fame. Billy was hurt, and George Flint took over playing in his spot and did a hell of a job on [defensive end] Ernie Ladd. We played so well out there, we shut them out!"

—Paul Maguire, punter

"We were following Lou Saban. He kept saying we could win. We just had a lot of good ballplayers. We didn't have that one person. There were guys like [Tom] Sestak that I'm sure should be in the Hall of Fame. We had a good defense. We had a good offense. It seemed like every week, somebody else would step up and get the job done one way or another. Whether it'd be Elbert Dubenion or Jack Kemp or Cookie Gilchrist or Wray Carlton, it was just an all-around good team. In fact, the '64 and '65 championship teams, there weren't that many different ballplayers on those teams. I think that was the big success. We just played well together, and the coaching was good, assistant coaches like Joe Collier and people like that. We were just a good team."

—Ron McDole, defensive end

"Well, I don't know how you get the right chemistry, but we had the right chemistry for a couple years there. The right players came along. I don't know what caused the chemistry, but it was there. I could say a lot of things, but who knows? Everything clicked. We had a lot of good players, and everything fell into place. We went [into the championship games] with the mind-set that we could win. We had a lot of confidence. We had no doubt that we could win the first year, and then the second year, we felt the same way."

—George Saimes, safety

"We were successful because of two things. One was that we had the best defensive team in football during that period of time. We were led by our defense. They were dominant! They gave up seven points in two [championship] games! The other point was that the offense was good enough to capitalize on the opportunity that the defense gave us. But when we talk about the Bills of that era, I'm proud that the offense was just good enough to get the job done, but our defense was awesome."

—Billy Shaw, guard

"I think it really started the year before. We finally got on a good track and started winning some games. Although we did lose a playoff game for our division to Boston in '63, '64 was when every-body sort of came together. It was what I consider more of a team effort than anything else. We had a good mixture. We had some folks that had played with other teams and other leagues and everything. And then we had some younger folks, too. I think Paul Maguire added quite a bit to our team as a punter and being able to see from the Chargers, who had a good run. Of course, he was telling everybody that we had more talent than the Chargers did. So I think he did a lot to build up the confidence of the team. Besides, all of his wisecracks and everything kept the team very loose. I think it was sort of a special time where we had a nice group of players that sort of came together and played with a lot of heart for each other. It was just more of a team effort than any-thing else."

—Mike Stratton, linebacker

"We just had an awful lot of talent. We had a great offensive line with Billy Shaw and Stew Barber and [Al] Bemiller. A tremendous defense! Our defense sometimes was our best offense! We had a nice, friendly rivalry between the offense and defense. If we got stalled on offense and couldn't do anything, when we were coming off the field, the defense would say, 'Don't worry, guys. We'll score for you if you guys can't score a touchdown.' And they did! They'd intercept passes and run them back for touchdowns. We just had some great guys and great coaches. That's what it was all about."

—Ed Rutkowski, wide receiver

"We had the horses, number one. That was an excellent team. Cookie Gilchrist running the ball, Bass and Dubenion at wide receivers, we had speed and an excellent offensive line. And defense. The defense was really great. But I think we finally jelled as a unit and, as they say, we went out there and kicked butts!"

—Ernie Warlick, tight end

chapter 8

2,003

O.J. Simpson rushed for a record 2,003 yards during the 1973 season.

Two Grand!

Reggie McKenzie: An outstanding offensive guard, a natural leader, and well, a visionary.

Following his rookie year, McKenzie had a thought cross his mind about what Buffalo's star running back O.J. Simpson, who had just led the NFL in rushing with 1,251 yards, and his offensive line teammates could do for an encore in 1973.

"Coming from Michigan [where McKenzie was a consensus All-American], we set goals in terms of running the football, and we put the expectations high," said McKenzie. "So right after the season, I got thinking. He gained what he gained with little or no blocking. If we get some blocking, there's no telling what he can do. Any time he touched the football, he could go the distance. And seeing the kind of speed that this guy had and the size he was, with any kind of blocking, we could gain 2,000 yards!

"He [Simpson] was talking about Jim Brown's [single-season] record [1,863 yards]. I said, 'Forget Jim Brown. Let's go do something nobody's ever done. Two grand!' He said, 'Come on, man.' I said, 'No, let's put it up there.' I said to the offensive line right before we got ready to go into the season, 'Listen, I kind of stuck my neck out there and said that we'd get O.J. 2,000 yards.' And I'll never forget Mike Montler saying to me, 'That's all right. We'll go after it.' And after seven ballgames, O.J. started believing."

And why wouldn't he? In the season opener, Simpson set an all-time league record with 250 yards during a 31–13 victory over the Patriots. He totaled 775 more yards over the next six games to reach 1,025 yards at the campaign's midpoint. And heading into the season finale against the Jets on December 16, in New York's Shea Stadium, Simpson had 1,803 yards, just 60 shy of Brown's record.

"Going into the last ballgame, O.J. was close to Jim Brown's record, but I said, 'Hey, man, forget that. Let's go get the whole enchilada. Let's go get two grand! Let's go get 2,000 yards,'" said McKenzie. "We would have an offensive linemen's meeting, particularly after Offense Day [when the week's game plan was installed during practice]. We would go over to Bruce Jarvis's house, and we'd get some film, and we'd have beer and sandwiches, and we'd sit there and look at the film and talk about what we were going to do that Sunday. We developed a bond that was special. Very special!

"We had Offense Day [prior to the season's final game against the Jets], and instead of going to somebody's house, we just went down to a meeting room and watched another can of film. After it was over, we all stood in a huddle and put our heads together and said, 'Let's go get this.' And we went to New York, and we got it!" In that game Simpson rushed for 200 yards to total 2,003 for the season. "You talk about the Electric Company, and you talk about that group and how special it was 30 years later. Two thousand three yards! The asterisk: 14 ballgames!"

The Electric Company Remembers 1973

"The longer it goes on, the more special it is. At the time, like all young kids, you don't appreciate or realize what you did. When I was at Michigan State, Eric 'the Flea' Allen was the running back, and we broke the national record. So I thought this was no big deal, I did this in college once before. As years went on, I thought no one's going to break that record. And truly, if O.J. had played now with all the spread offenses, with only five guys instead of eight on the line, he might go for 3,000 yards! I mean, we'd have even been better right now with that offense because he was absolutely incredible!"

—Joe DeLamielleure, guard

"It seemed like everything was jelling. We had a lot of guys that were starting to play together as a team, and O.J. showed some of his talent that he had from his prior years, in college and so forth. From an offensive-line standpoint, we had different guys that really could play and had taken to do what they said, 'Turn loose the Juice!' [Lou] Saban decided that we were going to run the ball, and Jim Ringo, who was an outstanding offensive-line coach, put in game plans that would feature our strength, running the ball. We did something that a lot of teams couldn't do. Well, 2,003 is one thing, but the other guys got over 1,000. We had over 3,000 yards that year.

"If you look at the whole picture, no great running back can do it without an offensive line. And no offensive line can make a guy that's not a great running back look great. A great offensive line can make a mediocre back gain yards, but the opposite is not true. In other words, to be a superstar, you've got to have a lot of talent. I would say what we had there was a lot of hardworking guys in the trenches that were all pretty good offensive linemen as far as running game and drive blocking and understanding the philosophy of moving the football. And then you had really the ultimate superstar as far as running backs in football at the time, that being O.J. Simpson.

"O.J. was the first running back in football to really bring his offensive linemen along with him. I know there are some wonderful running backs in the league that have done a lot of things for their offensive line since then, but I think he was the first that whenever he would end up getting an endorsement like sunglasses or cowboy boots or whatever, all the offensive linemen would get a pair of boots. All the offensive linemen would get a pair of sunglasses. The thing is, everybody got something out of that experience! It was just a magical time!"

—Dave Foley, offensive tackle

"There's no way an official is going to throw a flag [when Simpson passed 2,000 yards during the season finale in New York against the Jets]. I can't imagine Juice breaking the record and some guy calling holding unless you just grabbed somebody and threw him to the ground. It was really an exciting, exciting moment.

"After the game, Juice was leaving the field, and I was in the proximity of O.J., and the network guys came down and lassoed him. They wanted to do an interview with him. He said, 'Yeah, great.' It was set up in a boiler room, and there wasn't a whole lot of room in there. There were low-hanging pipes and things of that nature. Juice said, 'Well, let me get my boys, the offensive line.' They said they didn't have room for that, and Juice told them, 'If you don't have room for them, I can't do the interview.' They said, 'We'll make room for them.' I can remember going into that boiler room and ducking under the pipes. There wasn't a whole lot of room in there, but that's just the attitude of the entire team, the offense in particular. What made it click so much was that O.J. was to the point that, well, yeah, here's my glory, but he just flat out wasn't going to do the interview unless we were there."

—Mike Montler, center

"I was mainly a blocking tight end. And you had a guy like [Jim] 'Bubby' Braxton in the backfield, too. He was probably one of the greatest unrecognized fullbacks in the history of the NFL. Bubby could do it all. He could block, he could run, he could catch the ball. He was a great talent. Unfortunately, he wasn't healthy all the time. But when he was, there was nobody better. And we had Donnie Green and Dave Foley, who were Big Ten guys, and in the Big Ten back in those days, running was the paramount method of moving the ball. I think that had a lot to do with it. Yeah, it was kind of neat being able to be a historical rushing team. And not only did O.J. get his individual record, [but] we set the team record for yards."

—Paul Seymour, tight end

A Wideout That Blocks

Adjustments, even when done reluctantly, are a part of the game. In 1973 Buffalo's offense centered on running back O.J. Simpson, who on 332 carries would set an NFL record with 2,003 rushing yards. His backfield mates Jim Braxton and Larry Watkins added 908 yards on 206 carries. Rookie quarterback Joe Ferguson added 147 yards more. But receiver J.D. Hill, who was coming off a 52-catch Pro Bowl season, wanted to handle the pigskin, too.

However, since the game is played with only one football, and he realized it wasn't coming his way with any regularity, Hill became a blocker.

"[Veteran quarterback Dennis] Shaw is out. Ferguson is in. [Wide receivers] Haven Moses and Marlin Briscoe had already said, 'We're out of here.' They knew about Lou Saban and his running game. They knew Lou wasn't going to throw," said Hill, who would catch 23 fewer passes than in 1972. "I'm a young kid believing they're going to use my talents, and the next thing I know we're running the ball 40 times a game.

"There was just me and B.C. [Bob Chandler], and then they added Wallace Francis and some other receivers. I'm believing that, 'Hey, they're going to throw the ball. We want to win!' What I ended up finding out was that people were more excited about O.J. running 200 yards a game and trying to get 2,000 yards than we were about winning ballgames. It appeared that way anyway. We weren't trying to do everything to win."

He continued, "I got to the point where I became frustrated, and I got discouraged with the game of football. I was young and didn't know how to handle a lot of things, so my attitude began to change. We were running O.J. so much, and I wanted to catch the ball. Eventually I said, 'Hey, listen, I'm not going to get the ball, so I'm going to be an angry wide receiver. I turned into a wide guard and just started blocking. I became one of the best blocking wide receivers in the league, if not the best.

"It bothered me that they gave the line the 'Electric Company.' The whole team should have been the Electric Company. Everybody blocked! If I don't block the linebacker, he's going to shoot in there and mess up the pulling guard and O.J. doesn't get around the corner. I'm blocking guys that are 6'5" and 255, 260 pounds, and I'm at 190. And at times, they'd put me at double-tight, where I'd have to block with the tackles, Dave Foley or Donnie Green. It bothered me because I was a split end."

Hill's focus on playing without the ball wasn't unnoticed by his teammates then or later when they look back at what the Bills accomplished that season. "It was on an HBO special. Reggie

McKenzie said, 'If it wasn't for J.D. Hill, O.J. would never have gotten 2,003 yards,'" said Hill. "That was my trophy. I can't put it up on a mantle. I don't get to look at it, but I've got the picture of one of the greatest offensive teams ever assembled on my wall. When I look at that picture, I look at Dave Foley and Reggie McKenzie and Mike Montler and Joe DeLamielleure and Donnie Green, Paul Seymour, and Jim Braxton, O.J., and Bobby Chandler, Joe Ferguson. I know that I was a part of one of the greatest offensive units that was ever assembled. I loved the game, but I wanted to catch the ball. I wanted to win. I wanted to use my talents."

Fergy Hands Off to History

Four quarterbacks, including Bert Jones and Ron Jaworski, may have been chosen ahead of Joe Ferguson during the 1973 NFL draft, but none of those rookies had the opportunity to witness and participate in league history as he did.

Becoming Buffalo's starter during training camp after beating out Dennis Shaw, the Bills' quarterback the previous three seasons, Ferguson admits his passing performance was not as stellar as he would have hoped. By completing just 73 of 164 passes for four touchdowns and 10 interceptions, he was not in the running for many Rookie of the Year awards. He did, however, share the huddle and hand the football off to the NFL's Player of the Year, O.J. Simpson, who set a league record with 2,003 rushing yards.

"As nervous as I was, thank goodness I had a good running back to carry the load," laughed Ferguson. "It was the highlight of the year for me, being the quarterback and watching him do that and knowing that I was the guy that handed the football off for 99 percent of the plays. I think the fun part really was when it [Simpson breaking 2,000 yards] happened. In New York City, playing the Jets at Shea Stadium, the press, and how O.J. handled it after the game was outstanding. Those are all things that you remember. And the times in the huddle during that game, we knew

It was usually Joe Ferguson, here passing against the Redskins in 1977, who handed off the ball to O.J. Simpson to help him get his 2,003 yards in 1973.

he was close and knew we had a chance to do it. It was just amazing how the guys pulled together and helped him get the yards.

"No doubt, I was the luckiest player in the league that year. Actually the first couple years, because he took the pressure off and gave me a chance to learn the game and mature and carry the load. I was given a chance to come along, which a lot of guys don't have these days. It definitely made my career, the longevity of it, I'm sure."

chapter 9

Under Center

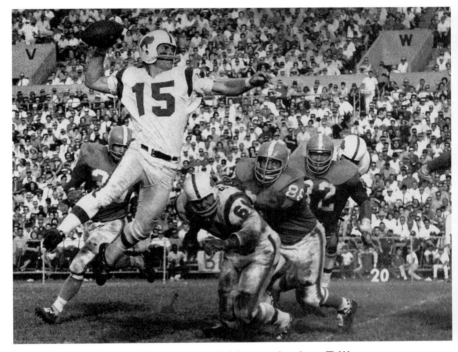

Although the Bills acquired him for $100, Jack Kemp (pictured here throwing a jump pass against the Houston Oilers in 1963) proved to be priceless as he became the star of the team and a phenomenal quarterback.

You Snooze, You Lose

The National Football League and the still-upstart American Football League were fishing in the same pool of college players during much of the 1960s. In 1963 the Bills selected Notre Dame quarterback Daryle Lamonica in the 24th round, 188th overall, while Green Bay chose him in the 12th round of the NFL draft. Appearance-wise, it seemed the Packers were more interested in the young signal caller than the Bills were. Buffalo, however, proved to be more persistent.

"Their [Green Bay's] scout had contacted me right after the draft and said he'd be back in a few days. Two or three weeks went by and no one contacted me," said Lamonica. "[Meanwhile] the Bills were contacting me daily and wanted to sign me. I had the East-West Shrine Game coming up, and they convinced me to sign a contract before I went and played that game so in case I got hurt, I'd still have a contract."

Quarterback? Check! Team leader? Check! Contract negotiator? Well, not so fast. "I didn't know what an agent was, and I was too embarrassed to call [former college teammate] Paul Hornung up in Green Bay and talk to him about it," Lamonica said with a laugh. "I can remember negotiating with Johnny Mazur, who was a receiver at Notre Dame and the receivers coach with the Bills. He was calling every day with the Notre Dame tie. They offered me a $1,500 signing bonus and an $11,500 contract. You've got to understand, I was from Fresno, California, and my mom was sending me $5 a week out of her beauty-shop tips. That was my date money and my spare money, and I got along pretty good.

"I went to [Notre Dame head coach] Joe Kuharich and said, 'Coach, this is the contract that I was offered.' And he said, 'That's a pretty good contract, and you ought to sign it.' I remember walking back to my dorm, and I thought, 'God, I'm worth more money than that.' So I called Johnny Mazur and said, 'Coach, I'm ready to sign, but before I go to the East-West Shrine Game, I've got to have more money. I need a $2,000 bonus and a $12,000 contract!' There was a long pause. He said [later that] he was laughing so hard he almost dropped the phone. He said, 'The contract's in the mail.'"

Lamonica continued: "So I sent it back and went to the East-West game. I was able to win the MVP. I had scouts coming up after the game saying, 'We'll give you a $100,000 bonus and a $100,000 contract to sign.' I'm going, 'What?' I didn't realize there was that much money in the whole world! But hell, with that [extra] $500 [from the Bills], I was able to end up buying a new Chevrolet Impala convertible."

"The Booing Turned to Cheering"

It cost just four cents to mail a letter in 1962. One could purchase three gallons of gasoline and get change back from a dollar. And as the Bills discovered, they could buy a quarterback named Jack Kemp off San Diego's waivers for $100.

Sidelined for all but the final four games of the 1962 campaign because of a broken finger, Kemp displayed evidence that Buffalo had spent its money wisely the following year when, during a three-game span, he passed for 869 yards, including two games when he totaled 300 or more yards.

In Kansas City on October 13, Kemp guided the Bills to a 35–26 win over the Chiefs. Two of his 12 completions resulted in touchdowns. The first was a 63-yard pass to rookie running back Roger Kochman in the third quarter, the only trip to the end zone in his five-game AFL career. And with 1:40 left in regulation, Kemp hooked up with wide receiver Elbert Dubenion on an 89-yard pass for his third touchdown reception of the young season.

"Oh, he was great," said Kemp, who passed for 300 yards. "He was the hardest-working man I've ever met in all my years of football. He had that Jerry Rice/Raymond Berry work ethic of incredible proportions. Very talented! Very fast! And not only hard-working, but indefatigable. Indefatigable! Just never would lose his driving spirit."

Less than two weeks later, on October 26, when the Bills hosted Boston, Kemp's driving ability was questioned by the 29,243 War Memorial Stadium faithful for a few anxious minutes in the fourth quarter.

"I will never forget that. It was 21–21, and we drove down the field and could have kicked a field goal to win the game," Kemp said. "We were in the baseball infield part, I would say, down inside the 10, and I called a tight-end look-in, and for some reason he got hit at the line of scrimmage and didn't get out. I didn't panic; I looked for another receiver. I started to drift back because I got a little pressure from the left side, my back side, and I couldn't find anybody. So instead of just throwing it away, I wanted to make something happen. And I really did! I tripped! From the infield to the outfield, the dirt to the grass was about an inch and a half of grass and I tripped and I fumbled. And they recovered!

"Oh, it was booing like you never heard in your life! It was unbelievable! They're still booing me! Oh, it was horrendous. I just felt humiliated for myself and the team. I'd taken a sure win and turned it into either a tie or maybe potentially a Boston victory."

Or maybe not! Buffalo's defense held the quarterback Babe Parilli–led Patriots offense and offered Kemp an opportunity to redeem himself.

"I'd been throwing a pass to Charley Ferguson, which was a check-off play called Blue-81. Eighty-one was the signal for Charley to run on a slant inside the corner," explained Kemp. "Their weak safety was playing way off, and [Nick] Buoniconti was at middle linebacker and knew me like a book. I mean, he knew me better than I knew myself. We're best friends, so I say this with a little bit of tongue-in-cheek, but we played each other three or four times a year. I threw one Blue-81 and it was completed for three or four yards, but I saw the weak safety reading my signals. They finally found out that Blue-81 was a slant.

"So I went in the huddle and said, 'Okay, you guys, there's not much time left. I'm going to call Blue-81, and I'm going to suck the safety in. I want you to block aggressively like you do on a slant. But after you block aggressively to keep the defensive guys' hands down, drop back into protection because I'm going to fake the 81. And Charley, you slant and do an up behind the weak safety.'

"I yelled, 'Blue-81! Blue-81!' right at Buoniconti, and I saw the weak safety start to inch up a little bit. So I went back and I pumped at about eight yards, the safety bit, and then I went back another two yards, and I must have thrown the ball before Charley even made his break. He broke into the clear and wasn't even looking when the ball was in the air, I swear to God, and it came down laces up, perfectly in his hands. I mean, it was just a picture play."

Kemp, who finished with 317 passing yards, continued. "And in the air—I swear to goodness—in the air, the booing turned to cheering. It was the most existential moment I've ever had in professional football. I've seldom even told the story to people because it's hard to understand. To hear booing in the air as the ball goes out and all of a sudden a little bit of silence and then cheering. It was a 72-yard touchdown play [with 28 seconds remaining, to win 28–21]. Oh, that was fun! And it saved me from being lynched going off the field. Buffalo fans do not like to lose."

Sunshine, Surf, Shula, and a Win

For 14 seasons, when the Bills traveled south to Miami, they headed back north with a loss. But on October 9, 1983, after winning 38–35 in overtime, the trip back to Buffalo was much more pleasurable.

Quarterback Joe Ferguson, who had been aboard 10 of those previous extra-long flights home, had the game of his career that afternoon in the Orange Bowl. He set the Bills' single-game records with 55 pass attempts, 38 completions, and 419 yards. He also tied his own single-game team record with five touchdown passes.

"Shoot, I don't know," Ferguson replied when asked what clicked for him that game. "We just wanted to beat Miami so bad.

It just felt good. I guess everything was going well for the team. We didn't turn the ball over, and that was usually the key when we played Miami. Usually whoever had the most turnovers lost the game, and usually it was us. Miami were the games of the year for us. It didn't matter, the Sun Belt and the Snow Belt. The whole team played well that day. Everything was clicking.

"You don't really have a feeling when you go out on the field. You just go out and do your job, and things fall in place. I didn't have a feeling that I was going to do a great job, I just went out and played one play at a time and whatever happens, happens. If it falls in place that day, it does."

With Joe Danelo's 36-yard field goal in overtime, the Bills' record went to 4–2. Miami dropped to 3–3 in rookie quarterback Dan Marino's first career start. "Maybe Joe had some motivation because of that, but Fergy was a great quarterback in his own right," said running back Joe Cribbs, who scored two touchdowns. "I really think that he probably doesn't get as much credit as he should get. Buffalo always had some great running teams when he was there, and he threw for a lot of yardage when you consider that most of the time he had to be handing the ball off to the likes of [O.J.] Simpson and [Terry] Miller. I think he had an exceptional career."

"I just remember that they were a good enough football team to come back, and we had to win it in overtime to show what a great football team we were," said Ferguson. "It was just a relief that we did win, and we won in Miami. That was the biggest thing. That was the best part about it, winning there."

Showdown in San Francisco

Jim Kelly had many special games under center for Buffalo. But when the Bills traveled west on September 13, 1992, to meet the San Francisco 49ers, he was spectacular! As was his counterpart, Steve Young.

Jim Kelly completed 22 of 33 pass attempts for an NFL career-high 403 yards and three touchdowns during this September 13, 1992, game against the 49ers at Candlestick Park.

Kelly completed 22 of 33 pass attempts for an NFL career-high 403 yards and three touchdowns, two to tight end Pete Metzelaars and one to running back Thurman Thomas. Young, meanwhile, passed for a career-high 449 yards and three touchdowns. The teams combined for 1,086 yards of offense, the fourth-highest total in league history. However, they did get into the NFL's record book by playing in a game where, for the first time, no punts were attempted by either team. The Bills won, 34–31, for their second of four victories to open the season.

"It was one of the most exciting games I've ever played in," said Kelly. "When you don't punt, either team, and you rack up as many yards as we did and wind up winning the game, we were very fortunate. Andre [Reed] was a key. Of course, Kent Hull was a key, and Thurman was a big key. But as far as the passing game, Andre was my man. He was the guy that I knew to go to in certain situations. I knew that he was the guy that not many could handle one-on-one on the inside. He was my go-to man, without a doubt!

"Pete was a guy that if I was ever in trouble, I knew I could look for that big ol' frame, and he was going to be there. He ran the best routes probably of anybody on the team. Not much as far as run after catch, but Pete was one of those guys who was Mr. Reliable. We were on the same page every single play."

As far as what turned out to be a Quarterback Challenge that was not a made-for-television event and did not involve trying to hit a target on a moving golf cart? "I remember playing him [Young] in the USFL, too," recalled Kelly. "'The Greatest Game That Nobody Saw' was the *Sports Illustrated* caption. We dueled out in Los Angeles, and the final score was like, 38–35, or something like that [actually 34–33]. They [L.A. Express] were beating us [Houston Gamblers] by three touchdowns, and we came back to beat them. Every time I played against Steve Young it was a battle."

The Comeback

Considering that Jim Kelly did not dress because of a knee injury and that star running back Thurman Thomas was out of the game with a hip pointer, Buffalo's chances to come back from a 35–3 second-half deficit against Houston in the AFC Wild Card playoff game on January 3, 1993, were slim to none. Slim won.

Behind backup quarterback Frank Reich, the Bills scored four touchdowns in less than seven minutes in the third quarter and were within four points heading into the final quarter. Buffalo took its first lead of the game with 3:08 left on the Rich Stadium scoreboard when Reich completed his fourth touchdown pass of the game on a 17-yarder to Andre Reed.

Following an Oilers field goal to send the game into overtime, Steve Christie secured the greatest comeback in NFL history with a game-winning 32-yard field goal. The Bills beat Houston, 41–38.

"Without question it's the game of my life," Reich told reporters. "I was pretty emotional when I got back to the locker room. I couldn't hold the tears back. Your thought is to take it one play at a time and don't try to force anything. When we scored to make it 35–24 late in the third quarter, that's when I thought it was really within reach."

Kelly was convinced, too. "In order to have a comeback like that you have to make some big plays. And I'll tell you, the poise that Frank showed out there, I don't think it can be matched. That was the greatest win I've ever been associated with, and I was on the sidelines."

chapter 10

Touchdown!

Jerry Butler, here getting tackled during a 28–27 victory over the Chargers in 1981, made his presence known early when he was drafted by the Bills in 1979. In just his fourth game, and playing with a slightly separated shoulder, Butler got 255 receiving yards on 10 catches, a remarkable four of which were for touchdowns.

Money in the Bank

The Bills returned from a two-game trip to California that opened the 1963 season with a pair of losses and free-agent wide receiver Charley Ferguson, who had been with Minnesota the previous year, on their doorstep.

"Believe it or not, I was a holdout for $1,500," said Ferguson. "That's peanuts in comparison to today, but they [the Vikings] would not give me the increase. And I was the leading receiver on the team! So then they released me at the last exhibition game. But there was an individual who was with the Bills [as the general manager] by the name of Dick Gallagher. Gallagher was a person who knew me [both were with the Browns in 1961]. So I was contacted by the Bills. I tried out and did extremely well, and Lou [Saban] offered me a contract, and I tried to get that $1,500 in that offer. He gave it to me, and believe it or not, I started at $7,500, so I went up to $9,000."

After five games as a backup to Bill Miller and playing on special teams, Ferguson cashed in on October 26, when Buffalo hosted the Boston Patriots. He caught a 72-yard touchdown pass with 28 seconds showing on the War Memorial Stadium scoreboard. The Bills won, 28–21.

"It was the first game I had the opportunity of playing in after I had joined the Bills. Right before the game was about to end, Lou and [assistant coach] John Mazur called me to the side, and they called [quarterback] Jack [Kemp] over, and they said, 'We want you to run a deep streak pattern,' which is an up pattern, just different terminology. I saw how they [the Patriots] were sagging off, trying to get to the outside of me, and I just kind of veered over a little more to the center of the field. It was just wide open. Jack read me extremely well. He threw it, and I made the catch, and it's all history after that."

The immediate history would show Ferguson back in the end zone after opening each of Buffalo's next two games with a touchdown: a four-yard reception in Denver and a 21-yard catch against the Broncos at home. The Bills won both games to go to 5–4–1.

Understandably, Ferguson was pleased with how things were progressing with his new team.

"I came over very confident, knowing that the NFL had been established and I had done well there, I thought. Coming to the new league, I was very, very confident. I just felt that I had a streak going, and things were going quite well for me. I felt good about it," Ferguson said. "That first game was really one of the fondest memories that I had, to really come in and have an impact and help win that game. That first touchdown pass coming in was real exciting to me. It also gave us a victory in order to end up playing in the playoffs that year."

Without Even Jumping

After five wins, one loss, and one tie in their last seven games, on November 13, 1966, the two-time defending AFL champion Bills hosted the New York Jets. And while there were certainly stars on Buffalo's roster, there was not a lot of star treatment.

"Our defensive unit always defended the field goals," said Jim Dunaway, a fourth-year defensive tackle. "If you were on the field when they were getting down close, you stayed there."

With a 7–3 lead in the fourth quarter, Buffalo was fortunate that Dunaway had indeed stayed there. Facing fourth down and a foot with a little more than 10 minutes remaining on the clock, the Jets chose to try to make it a one-point game and sent kicker Jim Turner in to attempt a 38-yard field goal. Well, the score changed, but on Buffalo's side of the scoreboard.

"I lined up on the outside of the guard and just drove inside to the hole. He had his weight to the outside, so I just went right through it. He almost gave me a hole," Dunaway said. "The ball hit me under my right arm and went to the left of the kicker and the holder. I was going that way anyway, so it bounced up to me a little bit, and I was lucky enough to pick it up and run along with it.

"I was about on the hash mark on the left side and went straight down the field, and I'm thinking somebody's going to catch me. I was hearing folks close behind me, and after the thing was over, I found out that it was Mike Stratton and John Tracey running along behind and doing interference for me. [Once in the end zone] I turned around and went to the sideline, and I kept the ball. I thought I earned that one. Of course, everybody was as happy about it as I was. I was hunting for some air."

Dunaway's 72-yard return, a team record that would stand for the next 13 years, and Booth Lusteg's extra point were the final points of the game, securing a 14–3 victory.

Leaving Broadway Joe in the Dust

Some players are upset when they are traded from one team to another. Tom Janik was not one of them. Joining the defending AFL champions may have had something to do with that.

"I was glad because I didn't like the coach at the time with the Broncos," said the safety, who was acquired by the Bills in 1965. "I liked Jack Faulkner, but then they let him go and they got another guy [Mac Speedie] there, and I didn't care for him at all."

After collecting a team-high eight interceptions in 1966, the Poth, Texas, native topped that the following season when he picked off a pass in four consecutive games, including three during a 44–16 victory against the Patriots on December 9. He finished with a league-leading 10 interceptions and earned a place in the AFL All-Star Game. "It was just one of those years. When you saw it coming and it came out right, you were there," Janik said. "You just had one of those years where everything works out right. The next year you might try the same thing, and it might just backfire on you, too."

New York's quarterback, Joe Namath, would likely attest that, in fact, it didn't backfire. Hosting the undefeated Jets on September 29, 1968, the winless Bills made Namath's afternoon miserable. Trailing 10–7 in the second quarter, New York was going for the lead when Janik stepped in front of a pass that was intended for Curley Johnson at the goal line and raced the interception untouched 100 yards for the touchdown.

"I loved every minute of that! When I saw Namath throw that pass, I said, 'Man, that's all she wrote,' and I took off," laughed Janik. "About the 30, I was laughing so hard because I turned around and looked, and he was limping and gimping, chasing me. I knew he couldn't run with his bad leg. [In the end zone] I threw the ball in the air and about 15 fans fought like crazy. After the game there was one guy that handed the ball back to me, and it looked like he was whipped on all day and all night long. But he had a smile from ear to ear."

Namath finished the game with five interceptions. In addition to Janik's return for a touchdown, Butch Byrd [53 yards] and Booker Edgerson [45 yards] returned picks to the end zone as well. The Bills won, 37–35, for their only victory in the 1–12–1 campaign.

Marlin the Magician's First Act

Less than nine months after Denver's rookie quarterback Marlin Briscoe passed for 335 yards and four touchdowns during a 34–32 victory over the Bills, on August 20, 1969, he appeared in Buffalo's training camp. As a wide receiver!

"After I had success my rookie year, I was not given the opportunity by [Broncos coach] Lou Saban to compete for the job. I asked for my release thinking that some other teams would give me an opportunity, but that wasn't the case," said Briscoe.

Discouraged, he gave the Canadian Football League a brief try but found he didn't enjoy that style of play. And so with the thought that they had witnessed his ability, Briscoe started calling AFL teams he had played well against.

"I'd almost beat the Oakland Raiders, and Coach [John] Rauch was there, and then he got the job in Buffalo. So when I called, he said that he didn't necessarily need a quarterback but needed some help at wide receiver. Well, I had never played wide receiver in my life on any level. I was always the quarterback.

"He did say they had drafted James Harris and that they had Jack Kemp and Tom Flores, but they were all injured. So when I got there, he had me throw and learn the position. I was actually playing two positions until those guys got healed, and then I was primarily learning the receiver slot," Briscoe said. "The only way I made it through that period was that I had negotiated in my contract that they not cut me until the last cut. I didn't want to come there knowing that I'd never played the position before and get cut immediately. So I studied films of Paul Warfield and Lance Alworth. And Bill Miller, who was the receivers' coach, took a special interest in teaching me the position. He was really diligent about giving me all the information that I needed to at least have an opportunity."

Briscoe's only chance to take advantage of that opportunity was on the practice field. He did not play during the preseason until the final game in Los Angeles. "I sat on the bench figuring they weren't going to put me in and that was going to be it. Well, we were losing and Coach put me in in the last 10 minutes of the game, and Jack Kemp just kept throwing me the ball and I just kept catching it. At the end of the game, I was the leading receiver, so they couldn't cut me.

"I ended up playing second string behind Bubba Thornton, and they had Haven Moses on the other side. Bubba was a track star from T.C.U., a 100-meter man, but he wasn't really a football player. So as I progressed week after week, I got the opportunity to get into games. First it was in the last quarter, then I would get in at halftime, and then it got to the point where Bubba would play a couple series and I would play the rest of the game."

When the AFL and NFL merged for the 1970 season, Thornton was gone and Briscoe was a starter. During Buffalo's first NFL victory on October 4 against the New York Jets, 34–31, he had four receptions for 120 yards and two touchdowns including the game-winning 25-yard catch in the fourth quarter. "I had success against [cornerback] Steve Tannen for some reason. I guess I had his number. But to be up there against the likes of Joe Namath and that crew was very rewarding to come out successful."

Briscoe would successfully find the end zone six more times during the season and become the team's first 1,000-yard wide receiver and Buffalo's only player selected for the Pro Bowl.

Hooked on Touchdowns

Through his first three seasons, Roland Hooks rushed for two touchdowns. He doubled that on September 9, 1979, when Buffalo hosted Cincinnati in the second game of the campaign. Behind Hooks's four touchdowns on just five carries, the Bills buried the Bengals, 51–24.

On the first play of the second half, Buffalo's linebacker, Shane Nelson, recovered a fumble at the Cincinnati 16. Four plays later, Hooks scored from three yards out. Later in the same quarter, with the Bills leading 24–17, Hooks capped a two-play, 57-yard drive with a 32-yard touchdown run to up the lead to 14 points.

On Buffalo's next possession, which occurred early in the fourth quarter, Hooks scored on a four-yard touchdown run. And following an interception by Bills linebacker Lucius Sanford less than two minutes later, Hooks found the end zone from 28 yards away for his fourth touchdown of the game.

"That was a game that I could do very little wrong," said Hooks. "It's kind of like being in a zone, whatever that is. That game, I guess I kind of was in the zone. For some reason, I made people miss. I remember looking at game films, and things seemed to be in slow motion while I was playing. I didn't remember doing some of the things that I had done. I was looking at it, and it was, 'I did that?' It was kind of amazing to watch. It was just a day to remember. It was just an unbelievable day."

The Butler Did It Four Times

It did not take long for Jerry Butler to demonstrate why he was the most coveted wide receiver in the 1979 NFL draft. On September

23, in just his fourth game with the Bills and playing with a slightly separated shoulder, he placed his name in the team's record book with 255 receiving yards on 10 catches. Four of the receptions were for touchdowns! Behind Butler and veteran quarterback Joe Ferguson's 367 passing yards and five touchdown completions, Buffalo beat its division rival New York Jets, 46–31.

"I had chicken wings for the first time on that Saturday [evening before the game]," said Butler. "The waitress said, 'How would you like them? Hot, medium, or mild?' I said, 'Hot.' I slammed the first one in my throat, and I thought I had horserad-ish! My nose was running, my eyes were watering. I thought when she said 'hot' she meant the temperature of the wings. I didn't know she was talking about the spice on the wings. I found out why you dip them in the blue cheese, to cool those suckers off!"

Come Sunday, Butler was as hot as the wings. After catching the first touchdown of his career a little more than five minutes into the second quarter, he brought the Rich Stadium crowd to its feet with only seconds remaining in the first half. Trailing 24–12 and from their own 25, Ferguson called Big Ben, Buffalo's name for the Hail Mary play. Seventy-five yards later, Butler was celebrating in the end zone.

"Like most of what you call Big Ben or Hail Mary plays, it's a last-second desperation-type play," Butler said. "The jumper was Frank Lewis. His position is to get down the field so he can get up and get a hand on it where he can tap it to the left or to the right. Joe put a lot of air under the ball, and the tip was turning over, and it came down. And Frank, I don't think he even got a chance to get his hand on it. They came over his back and actually tipped the ball themselves. I saw the ball falling back behind their stationary posi-tion, and I sprinted as fast as I could and caught it right before it hit the ground, and [I] took off running. We took a roll of the dice, and it rolled up in our favor, and it equated to seven points. They had a little bit more to think about going into the half, and we went in feeling a lot more upbeat about what we had just accomplished."

"Just a great effort on his part," said Ferguson. "We threw it up and there's just a hope. A throw and hope. You work on it in practice, naturally, which we did. A lot of teams don't work on it. They'd do it one time a week, and we'd do it 10. So we knew how to run the play. Then to have an athlete like Jerry that could run and jump, then you've got a big chance to make it."

Butler and Ferguson came up big again in the third quarter. First they connected on a 74-yard scoring play. "It was a route that adjusted to a fade to the outside," said Butler. "I don't remember if it was a blitz or not, but for some reason the coverage I got was a bump-and-run. If you're able to get away from that defensive back and you can make a move to get into good position and get leverage on him, you're in a pretty good situation to win. The ball was a little bit short. I remember slowing down a little bit and coming back inside, somewhat over the back of the shoulder. I think [Jets cornerback] Johnny Lynn pretty much stumbled and wasn't able to recover, to actually catch up with me. I swiped the ball and took it all the way in."

And on Buffalo's next possession, a 55-yard drive was capped off with a nine-yard touchdown reception by Butler on a slant play. "A pass from Fergy, I would call a 'frozen rope,'" Butler said. "He would zip that thing. People don't realize, when you're in the red area, as a receiver, you don't even see the quarterback sometimes. The ball just comes out of there. That's what practice is all about. You start to anticipate the timing. Being a rookie coming into the league, it was kind of a welcome party, and it was a good boost for my career."

Big Ben Beats the Patriots

It ain't over 'til it's over. Those six words were seldom more appropriate than when the Bills faced New England at Rich Stadium on November 22, 1981. With no timeouts and trailing 17–13, Buffalo had 35 seconds remaining in the fourth quarter to travel 73 yards for a touchdown. Just getting in range for Nick Mike-Mayer to attempt a field goal was clearly not an option.

The Bills lined up for what they called 90 All Go. The pass play's first option was for quarterback Joe Ferguson to look for the halfback—in this case, veteran Roland Hooks, who was in for an injured Joe Cribbs—down the middle of the field. "Everybody took off," said Hooks. "The outside receivers were supposed to clear and get the defensive backs downfield and put pressure on the safeties. I was supposed to split the seam and get behind the backers, which I was lucky enough to do. The ball was slightly overthrown, and I had to dive, and I caught it with my fingertips. It was a pretty big catch."

It was indeed. The 36-yard gain left Buffalo at the Patriots' 36-yard line. But with the much-needed time still running, Ferguson quickly threw a pass out of bounds to stop the clock with just 12 seconds remaining. As the Bills huddled, they were equally excited and confident.

"We'd got the ball deep in our own territory when the series started, so we were moving the ball," Hooks said. "I know we didn't have a lot of time, and Big Ben was a desperation last play. But we had made up so much ground in a short period of time, and we probably would have had two shots. I don't ever remember playing a game, particularly a close game, where we have a chance of winning, thinking, 'We can't do this.' Particularly on offense, we were pretty confident that we could get the job done."

The Big Ben play that Hooks referred to called for receivers Jerry Butler and Frank Lewis to line up beside him and sprint to the end zone relatively close together to try to haul in Ferguson's pass among New England's defenders.

"Frank was in the middle; he was the leaper. Jerry was on the outside, and I was on the inside. In practice Joe got most of the work, but we had run it so many times, I was familiar with the play. I don't know that it ever worked in practice," Hooks said with a laugh. "But we had had some success with it. Jerry actually caught one against the Jets [in 1979].

"I was feeling real tired. When the signals were called and the ball was snapped, I just took off downfield and was trying to space myself because we knew that the ball was going to go up the middle to Frank. I was just trying to get in a good position; if it was deflected, I would be in a position to catch it."

Hooks was in the right position at exactly the right time. He cradled the ball, which had deflected off Patriots linebacker Mike Hawkins, for the touchdown with only five seconds left in regulation.

"I was lucky enough for things to work out that way. We were all lucky enough for it to work out that way," said Hooks. "I was mobbed in the end zone. I was standing up when I caught the ball, and the next thing I knew, someone had stepped on my back, and I don't know how many guys were on top of me. But looking at the film, there were quite a few on the pile. I had the breath knocked out of me. I think I had landed on the ball. I was just happy that I made the catch and that we came up with a win that we needed."

First Game, First Catch, First Touchdown

Don Beebe, Buffalo's top draft choice (third round) in 1989, possessed bulletlike speed. But during the first two games of his rookie season, the wide receiver was left in the holster, so to speak, and did not play.

"We weren't in the K-Gun offense then, and I was the fourth receiver," said Beebe, a third-round selection. "After the second week, [quarterback Jim] Kelly went into Coach Levy's office and said, 'Hey, listen, I want Beebe on the field.' And lo and behold, they cut Chris Burkett, and he signed with the Jets. So I got an opportunity because of Jim to play in my first game, which was against the Houston Oilers at the Astrodome on September 24. I felt very honored that Jim would go in. I was a high pick and could run, and I think Jim wanted to utilize that ability because he loved to throw it deep, as every quarterback does. Especially Jim! He wanted to throw it deep, and the first opportunity that he got, he did!"

That he did. During the Bills' first possession of the second half, the wide-eyed No. 82 was in the huddle and heard Kelly call

Don Beebe accomplished a rare feat when he scored his first touchdown on his first catch during his first NFL game.

a run play. "I remember going up to the line of scrimmage and [cornerback] Cris Dishman was bump-and-run on me. He was talking trash, and it was all in fun, but he was saying stuff like, 'Hey! I hear the white boy can run! Let's see it! Let's see it!' I was scared to death," Beebe laughed. "So on third down, I'm in the huddle and it's a pass play. I'm supposed to run a post-corner. Jim looks at me and says, 'Beebs, if Dishman's pressing you again, just take him! Take him deep! I don't care what route you've got, run by him!' So I'm thinking, 'Oh, God, here we go.' I go up to the line of scrimmage and Dishman's talking trash again, and I beat him for a 63-yard touchdown."

It was Beebe's first NFL catch, first touchdown, and well, the first time he was mugged by jubilant teammates.

"Oh, it was euphoria. You watch a guy score a touchdown, and you'll see a couple guys come up and high-five him or pat him on the butt or whatever," said Beebe. "You watch that game, and the first guy that was there was Andre [Reed]. He came in and tackled me! He hit me, and I actually hurt my shoulder, he was so excited. Then everybody on that team was down on that field congratulating me. I couldn't believe it. And then after I got to the sideline and everybody stopped saying congratulations and all that, I actually sat there on the bench and was reflecting on what just happened. I'm thinking, 'Oh, my God! I just scored a touchdown!' I knew that my whole family was at home watching because I told them I was going to play on third downs. It was a cool moment for me as everything quieted and I was just sitting there alone on the bench.

"And this is the funny part about the story. I remember the next time I come out of the huddle, I'm walking up to the line of scrimmage and Dishman comes up to bump-and-run, and he says, 'Dang, I guess the white boy *can* run!' and he backed up about four or five steps."

Even if word spread around the league that the "white boy" could indeed run, it would not have mattered. Five games later against the Dolphins, Beebe was on the receiving end of another 63-yard touchdown pass. This one was from Kelly's backup, Frank Reich.

"During the course of that game, I remember Frank kept saying, 'Hey, Beebs! I promise you, we're coming to it. I know you can take him. I'm still waiting for the right opportunity to audible to it.' And sure enough, we got the play called. Frank threw; there've been some great passes thrown my way, but that ball was so perfect. What you want on a deep ball is your receiver to actually accelerate through the ball. And that ball couldn't have been placed more perfectly. I really accelerated and reached out and just caught the nose of it. It was really kind of an easy thing, I'll be honest with you; it was just a great throw."

You Can Go Home Again!

Sure, he grew up in Cleveland, but Darryl Talley was not a Browns fan. Nevertheless, when the Bills traveled to Cleveland Stadium to meet the Browns on November 4, 1990, the eighth-year veteran linebacker collected a few souvenirs from his hometown team. Not hats, shirts, or even a plastic dog bone, but two interceptions and the first touchdown of his career, helping Buffalo win its sixth straight game, 42–0.

Cleveland, having lost six of its last seven games, had Mike Pagel playing at quarterback instead of Bernie Kosar. However, the Bills evidently did not care who was calling the signals and led, 21–0, in the second half, when Talley made Pagel's afternoon a little less comfortable with the two picks.

"The first one was tipped up in the air, and I just outjumped everybody for it," said Talley. "The second interception, I thought was kind of stupid on Pagel's part. They ran the play one time with [tight end] Ozzie Newsome in the game. The same formation and the same backfield set. They completed the ball on one side of the field, and then two plays later, they came back and tried to run the same play to the other side. The cadence and everything sounded so familiar to me, I looked at him and asked, 'Do you think I'm stupid?'

"The ball was being thrown to my brother on a Big Dig route, and I just ran and jumped in front of it. I started to run down the field, and as he started to close on me, [safety] Dwight Drane came up and hit my brother square in the face and knocked the snot out of him. I just ran the rest of the 60 yards."

That was something else that made the game memorable for Talley. While there were "tons" of family members in the crowd, Darryl was not the only Talley on the field. His younger brother, the aforementioned snot-deprived John, was a first-year tight end with the Browns.

"Being from Cleveland and playing against the Browns and my younger brother, who I taught to play tight end outside in the drive-way.... That was one of my first games on the field there in Cleveland. I never got to play in high school there, so I was thrilled; I was excited about playing there. Especially playing against my brother! It was very special. Not that many people get to play against their brother at that level."

Can't Spell Thurman without MVP

Buffalo's 1991 season-opening 35–31 victory over its archrival Miami Dolphins could have been a sign that running back Thurman Thomas was going to enjoy a special and successful year.

By rushing for 165 yards (including a seven-yard scoring run) and catching eight passes for 103 yards (including a 50-yard touchdown toss from Jim Kelly), Thomas became the first player in Bills history to top the century mark for rushing and receiving in the same game.

The fourth-year veteran went on to total 1,407 yards on the ground and 631 yards in the air—2,038 total—to lead the league in combined yards from scrimmage for the third consecutive season. He was recognized as the NFL's Most Valuable Player that year. The following season, with 2,113 combined yards, Thomas became the only player to lead the league for four consec-utive seasons.

"I think it was my coach, the great Elijah Pitts," Thomas said. "My first couple of years, he taught me the ins and outs of professional football life on and off the field. I think with him playing in Green Bay in those championship years [1961–1962 and 1965–1967], I used his experience, his knowledge, to get more adapted to the game.

"I knew the game, but there were certain things that he taught me. The number one thing was that you don't need to be running around a lot. You need to rest your body because you're going to handle the ball 25 to 35 times a game. At that point in time, I stopped traveling a lot during the off-season. I basically stayed off my feet. The only time was when I worked out. I just rested. I think going into that year that was the key point for me."

Sharing with the Family

Coming off their first AFC title, the Bills made history again in 1991 when, for the first time, they had two players collect 1,000 receiving yards. Andre Reed led Buffalo with 1,113 yards, and James Lofton added 1,072 yards, his highest total in six seasons. Both were named to play in the Pro Bowl—Reed's fourth consecutive time and the eighth trip for Lofton.

"I just got more into the offense," said Lofton. "If you look at the playoff numbers from the year before, those are kind of reflected on what I was able to do the next regular season. The quarterback got a little more confidence in me because it was not like a coach on the sideline was calling our plays; Jim Kelly was calling them on the field. And people were probably trying to stop Andre Reed a little more, so that allowed me to catch some passes."

One of those passes was a 27-yard touchdown toss from Kelly during a 24–13 win over the Jets on December 1, the ninth straight victory over the division rivals. It was a memorable catch because he could share it. Well, kind of. "My oldest son, David, was probably seven at the time, and he and Pete Metzelaars's and Jim Ritcher's sons normally sat pretty high up in the stands, but this game, they were down in about row three or four. After I caught the ball, I remember running over and handing it to him. I remember thinking, this is the ball that he will take home and put in the trophy case. I had never done anything like that before," Lofton said. "After the game I did a bunch of interviews and came out, and my wife was there with my other son, Daniel. So we walk out to the parking lot, and there David is with Metzelaars's son and Ritcher's son, and they're throwing this ball around. It's about as dirty as it can get! It's wet and scuffed up and everything! I was thinking that he'd take it home and make a trophy out of it, and it never dawned on me how excited the boys would be to have a ball that was actually used in a game. I realized how fortunate I was to get to have my sons get to watch me play and just how much fun they were getting out of watching us play."

The Big Guy Steps Up

During the 1990 and 1991 campaigns, tight end Pete Metzelaars stopped blocking long enough to post 15 receptions for 114 yards. But when the two-time defending AFC champion Bills traveled to San Francisco on September 13, 1992, the 6'7", 254-pound veteran became a larger-sized Andre Reed and caught four of Jim Kelly's passes for a career-high 113 yards and two touchdowns.

The first time Metzelaars found the then–Candlestick Park end zone was early in the third quarter with Buffalo behind, 24–13, when he scored on a 53-yard play. And, well, it was not easy.

"I barely got in," he laughed. "Actually, it was one of our real basic plays that we ran six or seven times a game. My part was to just run as fast as I could, which wasn't real fast, and get out of the way. But for some reason Jim said, 'Hey, Pete, just be ready.' He just had a sixth sense in the middle of the game where he would just feel like something was going to work, something would be open. And more times than not, it would work out just the way he thought it was going to. So I released and got down the field a little bit, looked around, and there was the ball. I caught it and made the free safety miss, or he just missed, and got to the end zone. Barely!"

Less than six minutes later, Metzelaars was back in the end zone finishing off a 24-yard scoring play that put the Bills on top, 27–24. They'd go on to win, 34–31. "That was actually about the same thing," said Metzelaars. "It was the same pattern. I don't know that Jim said to be ready, but it was one where I was clearing down the field and he got some pressure and started scrambling. I just broke it off to the right and there was nobody there, and he threw me the ball for another touchdown.

"It was a Ping-Pong match, a tennis match, whatever you want to call it. It was just back and forth. They'd go down and score, then we'd go down and score. That's the way it went throughout. It was an incredible game."

The First One's Worth Seven

A player's first career interception in the NFL is always memorable—more so when that first interception turns into his first and, as it would turn out, only career touchdown. And even more so when it's off a former teammate making his initial return to Orchard Park after 10 seasons with the Bills. Fourth-year safety Kurt Schulz collected that first pick during the 1995 home-opening 31–9 victory on September 10 over the Carolina Panthers.

"I was coming down in short coverage and just reading the quarterback's eyes," Schulz said. "We had a great rush, and I jumped in front of Frank Reich's ball and ran it in 32 yards for a touchdown."

While Schulz may not have been widely recognized as a pass thief during his first three seasons, that began to change after returning Reich's pass to the end zone. He came up with five more interceptions during the course of the season, and four of his team-leading six picks were converted into points.

"I think whenever you have a great pass rush and you have all the guys around you, you trust them to do their responsibilities. A lot of the time, the free safety is able to make big plays on other people's pressure and fulfilling their side of the play," said Schulz, who was named second-team All-AFC by UPI. "So a lot of times, it's just a matter of anticipation and reading the quarterback. I think one of the areas that I excelled in was getting a little jump on the play, especially when there's a lot of pressure on the quarterback. They have a tendency to stare a little bit more, and the free safety can take more liberties and anticipate a little bit more."

Special-Teams Ace Also Catches

Steve Tasker: special-teams star, locker-room leader, media go-to guy. And in 1995, after a series of injuries to his teammates, he became a starting receiver and notched the first multi-touchdown game of his 11-year career (10 with Buffalo) in St. Louis on December 10, helping beat the Rams, 45–27.

"I knew I was going to [start] early in the week because there was just nobody else to put in. Everybody was injured, and I got pushed into the lineup," Tasker laughed. "I was kind of excited because it was the first time I was ever going to get introduced, and I told my wife to tape it.

"I knew I was also going to return punts in that game. I was actually leading the league in punt returns, and I was having a good time doing that. Plus, I was going to play wide receiver. I was always very happy playing special teams, but I never really realized how fun it would be to be out there so much, be in the game and contribute in different ways. So I was really excited about the chance just to be out there and play.

"We went in running an offense we'd been running for a lot of years, and the reason [Jim] Kelly wanted me in was because I was there when the thing was invented. I started playing, and he liked the way I ran the routes. He always did because I thought a lot like he did, and he started throwing me the football."

One of those throws came during the Bills' first possession of the second half. Leading 21–13, Kelly capped off an 80-yard, 10-play drive with a six-yard touchdown pass to Tasker.

"It was a quick route, and it wasn't there at the beginning, so I got to the back of the end zone and started running across, and Jim gunned it in," said Tasker. "I knew when he threw it I was going to get whacked if I could catch it. I caught it, and just as I did, the DB hit me really good. I ended up being like six yards out the back of the end zone. He got me good, but I remember I had a nice spike after that."

Tasker found the end zone again after hauling in a 28-yard pass from Kelly during Buffalo's next possession. "I ran a corner route. Jim never saw me catch it. He was on his back! He hung in there and took the hit and got the ball out," Tasker said. "I was running and looking over the wrong shoulder, and Jim threw it right over the top of my head. It was a great throw. Then I was just able to weave inside the pylon to get in the end zone, and we got the touchdown. I'm really surprised when I look back on it that I made the catch. It was funny because they had a shot of Jim on the ground, and I think he knew it was a pretty good catch. He and the defensive lineman who had whacked him were both laying there, and they both look up and turn to where the ball was thrown, and Kelly put both fists up in the air and goes, 'Yeah!' Jim told me the defensive lineman just said, 'I can't believe he caught that!'"

Tasker finished the game with four catches for 54 yards and two touchdowns. He, however, almost made a third trip to the end zone. "I should have had [another] one, too," recalled the receiver. "Jim called a play that we had run earlier, and he told me to run a different route on the play. On the earlier play, we got a nice gain on it. Then we ran the same play and I ran the change that he told me earlier instead of running the regular play, and Jim had to throw an incompletion. He was ticked at me, I remember."

chapter 11

Memories of the Super Bowl Seasons

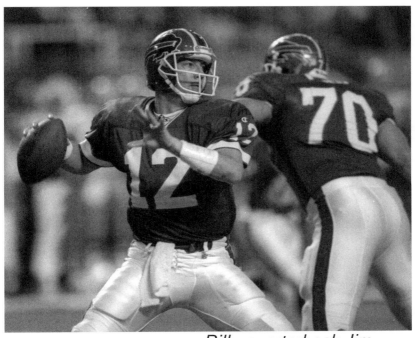

Bills quarterback Jim Kelly looks to pass the ball during Super Bowl XXVIII against the Dallas Cowboys at the Georgia Dome in Atlanta, Georgia, on January 30, 1994.

1990: 13–3: Super Bowl XXV:

New York Giants 20, Buffalo 19

1991: 13–3: Super Bowl XXVI:

Washington 37, Buffalo 24

1992: 11–5: Super Bowl XXVII:

Dallas 52, Buffalo 17

1993: 12–4: Super Bowl XXVIII:

Dallas 30, Buffalo 13

"There's no question in my mind, and now that I'm a [high school] head football coach, I truly understand what makes a team successful. Talent doesn't win. And I'm not taking anything away as far as talent because talent-wise we were extremely loaded. But what wins is just camaraderie. You like your coach; you like the whole atmosphere that you're in. I've got to tell you, we were family then. People still talk about that team! People from other teams talk about that team! I've been at a lot of different functions since I retired, and guys will come to me and say, 'Man, you guys had something special, didn't you, in Buffalo?' And I'll say, 'Yeah. We did.' And what made it special was the community—our general managers, John Butler and Bill Polian, and our head coach, Marv Levy.

"John Butler, God rest his soul, was one of the great human beings in the NFL. I would put Polian in that category. And without a doubt, my number one guy is Marv Levy. I can't tell you enough good things about Marv Levy. He is an amazing guy. I wish I could be half the man Marv Levy is."

—Don Beebe, wide receiver

"For a team to do that four years in a row, it's unbelievable! I know when we went in the '93 season to Super Bowl [XXVIII] and unfortunately lost, how much it took out of me personally. How bad you feel for losing. It's not only mentally draining, but physically draining. And then it wears on you during the next season. And for a team to do that four years in a row, it's amazing that an NFL team did that during this day and age. It says a lot for not just the players, but also for the coaches. I'm sure you always heard Marv Levy when he said, 'The guys are resilient.' It's a resilient organization from top to bottom. From the owner, Mr. Wilson, to all the players and the people who work in the front office! Everyone associated with the Bills organization."

—Bill Brooks, wide receiver

"Marv [Levy], Bill Polian, and John Butler, the last years; they weren't afraid to keep guys around. And that was the pre-cap era.

Really from the get-go, Bill Polian was aggressive in keeping and getting guys. Once he got a guy on Plan B or however he got them, he was going to keep them. The secret was to keep that chemistry and, by doing that, to keep a pretty steady roster. Every year, every team had changes, but he kept a core of guys, and that was the big thing.

"The other thing was the desire that the team had to come back and make another appearance and to try to ultimately win the Super Bowl. Had they won the first or the second one, would there be that drive to come back? It's so difficult to make it to the Super Bowl year in and year out. You look at what the Steelers did to defend their title [in 2006]. It's not that easy. Things fell apart for them. They were Super Bowl champs, but it seemed like when they won, they were pretty content with the whole thing. I saw sort of a lack of drive from them. From their head coach all the way down. Whereas in the Bills' case, not having won, there's always that itch or that drive. There's something propelling each guy individually and the team as a whole to go back and see if you can't do it again and this time get the big ring and the Lombardi Trophy!"

—Steve Christie, kicker

"[The first Super Bowl, XXV, was] probably a little more [than what was expected]. I played for a national championship [at Penn State] before, and that was a pretty big deal. But I would say [the Super Bowl hoopla is] times three. It's an event! And it's a hell of a lot more fun for the patrons than it is for the players. But I think we were the best team that first year."

—Shane Conlan, linebacker

"I don't remember a whole lot about it [Super Bowl XXV] because you get caught up in it and you're like, 'Hell, I can't believe we're in the Super Bowl!' We knew we were good enough. You're playing during the Persian Gulf War, and the intensity was just amazing. We were playing in front of the world, and I'm a part of it. And I'm proud to say that was one of the best games that I played in the NFL, going against [New York's] Lawrence Taylor and some of the other guys. You wish you can remember more, but you can't. But it was a lot of fun. That's the hardest one for me to watch on the TV replays because obviously that one hurts more than any of the others because we did have a chance to win it in the end. We just couldn't come through."

—John Davis, guard

"[The Super Bowl teams were successful] for a lot of different reasons. I think one of the biggest reasons started with Coach Levy. I think that he had us well prepared. Not only did he have us well prepared, but I think he had his coaching staff well prepared. Everyone got along. I think the parties that we had at Jim's [Kelly] house after the games and the different things we did out in the public together helped generate a lot of that excitement. It was just that time of year, just that aura that everything was coming together. I think that being able to have that type of a vision and being able to have that type of cohesiveness as a team, that's what made us so good. You've got to have cohesiveness as a team! You don't have to love each other, but you've got to be able to get along with each other and you've got to be willing to help one another. When another guy's not picking up his slack, not only do you help him, but you tell him that he's got to pick it up, too. They just put together a special group of guys."

—Kenneth Davis, running back

"My first Super Bowl [XXVI] was in Minneapolis, which is about three hours from my house, so it was kind of like a homecoming. Trust me, there were no extra tickets. I used every ticket I had, that's for sure. I didn't know what to expect. I knew we were going to play a game and it was going to be televised, but I just didn't realize about all the marketing and how everybody wanted a piece of your time during Super Bowl week. Whether it was shoe contractors or, I remember in Minneapolis, the Zubaz people. Back in the early '90s, that was the hot item. They wanted to get their stuff out so people could see it, so they were giving it to everybody.

Some players went to their factory and came back with as much as they could carry.

"I wasn't there for the building blocks of what propelled the Bills to those four Super Bowls. The building blocks of those teams were the same guys, the continuity, and that happened in the late '80s. I got to experience the best parts of it, which were the Super Bowls. The one thing that I remember in all those years with all the core guys being together is no matter how far we were down, there was always something extra. They talk about the 12th man; the 12th man to me was that no matter how far we were down, we knew we'd find a way to win. It was just a sense. I can't explain it any more than that. They talk about chemistry and all those things that make teams great; well, we had a lot of physical talent, we had good offense, good defense, good special teams, but there was something extra. Marv Levy had a lot to do with that, too. He kind of was the calming, soothing father figure for the players. I think that did a lot for our play on the field as well."

—Phil Hansen, defensive end

"[That first Super Bowl, XXV, was] probably more than I expected. Everything went so fast it was a blur. We win the AFC Championship Game, and the next thing I know I'm in Tampa. With the media and the fans and families, it was just so confusing. You were almost relieved the day of the game. As hard as it is to play the game of football and especially a Super Bowl, it was a relief! I never dreamed that there would be anything like that.

"We were fortunate enough to get to four straight Super Bowls in a time before free agency. You had a chance to groom young players in a need where you had maybe an older guy that was getting to the end of his career. Now you sign him to a three- or four-year contract, and in the fourth year when he really matures, free agency takes him away from you. We didn't have to worry about that. I don't think with the way things are structured in the National Football League today, you could keep a core of players together like we had in the late '80s and early '90s."

—Kent Hull, center

"I think Marv [Levy] put it best: 'I don't think it's schemes or coaching styles, you just have to have a bunch of talented, hardworking guys that go out and play well together.' There was a lot of camaraderie on that team, and we had a lot of butt-kickers, a bunch of guys that could go out and flat play!"

—Henry Jones, safety

"I tried to remove myself from all of the distractions. As far as the hoopla was concerned, it lived up to expectations. There's a lot of excitement surrounding the game. There was a lot going on [prior to Super Bowl XXV] because of the war in Kuwait and Desert Storm and all that. But that was kind of a whirlwind year because, if you recall, they didn't have a two-week delay before the game. They only had one week between the AFC Championship Game and the Super Bowl. Sunday morning, you're preparing to play for the AFC championship, and Monday morning you're in a plane on your way to Tampa. It was exhausting, really. And once I got there, I just tried to remove myself, stay in the motel and watch film and get prepared. But there were a lot of distractions, and I think the team that can be more successful is the team that can eliminate the distractions."

—Mark Kelso, safety

"I've gotten a chance to measure it against others that I've worked at as a broadcaster and then being at the others. I think the further you get removed from playing in one, you realize how big of a deal it is, the historical significance within the game that we play and the weight that it takes on and the heroes that it makes for that moment and that season. I don't think that [going to four straight Super Bowls] will be repeated. It was tough enough to win your division. That's why I think that group of players and that team will go down as one of the best teams in NFL history."

—James Lofton, wide receiver

"[That first Super Bowl, XXV,] was an incredible experience, the emotion of the whole thing. It was during Desert Storm, and all that stuff was going on. So that was all stacked up on it also. It was a great time, but at the same time that whole week went by it seemed like in about 12 hours. It just flew by! You kept going, 'Wait! Slow down! I want to enjoy this a little more.' [Four consecutive AFC championships] I think is something we can hang our hat on. And although we did not win the Super Bowl, which was our goal and continues to be every player's goal, we can say we went four times in a row. No one's ever done that, and no one probably ever will do that. It's something that we're very proud of. Yeah, we came up short, and that's all you can say. But we achieved and accomplished a lot, and we're proud of what we accomplished."

—Pete Metzelaars, tight end

"Never experiencing anything like that, it was all right. I enjoyed it for a lot of different reasons, for my teammates, my coaches. I just wish the outcome could have been a lot better. Even though we didn't win, all of us wanted to go out and play hard for each other. There's one thing about the team: we really cared for each other. All of us are still friends. We might not talk a lot, but we're still friends to the end. I wouldn't trade it for the world. I enjoyed playing for Buffalo and I enjoyed working for Mr. Wilson. He's one of the better owners in the NFL."

—Nate Odomes, cornerback

"I didn't get to play a lot [in that first Super Bowl, XXV]. I played in short-yardage and goal-line situations. During the season I played so much, and once the playoffs rolled around, I didn't get to play as much as I had hoped. And then the Super Bowl, it was a neat experience to be there, but we didn't have a week off between like they do so often now. So you really just went right from the championship game; we're on a plane and there we are. It was fun, but I was so caught up in being a rookie in the NFL, the Super Bowl was just one more event.

"I don't think anybody's going to do that [go to four straight Super Bowls] again. Not in this era. And let's face it, in the pre–salary cap free-agency era, nobody had done it, so I don't think anybody can get it done again. It's too hard to keep your nucleus together, too hard to keep players hungry. A lot of credit goes to Marv Levy for doing that. He kept the team on an even keel, yet always hungering for that next step."

—Glenn Parker, guard

"Number one, we were a highly confident team. My last few years were so different in a lot of ways than those Super Bowl years. During the Super Bowl years, we as a team, as a whole from top to bottom, went into every game and honestly in our hearts knew we were going to win. That was the mentality that we had. There are four areas of football. There's offense, defense, the kicking game, and special teams. The great players we had on offense— Jim Kelly, Thurman Thomas, Andre Reed—they knew we had that covered there. The same way with the defense. They knew that whatever happens on this kickoff or that punt, we've got good players over there. And we did during those years! We had a lot of really high-caliber players: Dwight Drane, Jamie Mueller, Hal Garner, and Carlton Bailey. You can just go down the list. Each area of football, they knew that the other guys have their back."

—Mark Pike, special teams

"There were a lot of keys. I think the main key was that we wanted to stay together. With free agency and everything that's going on now, a lot of teams aren't staying together. A lot of players are moving around. We wanted to stay together, and we knew that we had something special if we just worked at it and got to know each other on the field. That was probably a big reason why a lot of the guys did want to stay with the Bills at that time. We had the nucleus of a team that could be very success-ful, and we were. I played with some Hall of Fame players, and in order to be a Hall of Fame player, you've got to have some people around you also.

"We had a good quarterback, a good running back, and a good defensive end. And then we had guys that played a certain kind of role for our team that put us over the top. That was the special part about it, that anybody on any given Sunday could play well and could contribute."

—Andre Reed, wide receiver

"The Super Bowl experience is probably third in my life as to what are the best things that ever happened to me. The first two are my two kids being born. To walk out through that tunnel on Super Bowl [XXV] Sunday and we're in the Gulf War.... When those planes flew over your head with the one missing, you got chill bumps on your arms and legs. The hairs on your arms stood up when you walked out on the field. And then you've got millions and millions of people looking at you, watching you play that game. And you think about that. 'Where else would you rather be than right here, right now?' to quote Marv.

"I look back at it as being a member of one of the gutsiest and the most resilient football teams I've ever seen or been around. I've never seen so many people that refuse to give in or refuse to bow down or be told what they can do or what they can't. Even when nobody wanted us to come back, we were like Jason! We just showed up."

—Darryl Talley, linebacker

"We didn't really get a chance to experience the hoopla and the excitement in Buffalo because about 12 to 14 hours after the championship game against the Raiders was over, we were on a plane [to Tampa for Super Bowl XXV]. We never really got a chance to feel the excitement that the city was feeling. So that was kind of a downer that we missed out on all of that. But other than that, when we got down there, the game and everything was great! All except the part where we lost.

"The fact that we went to four straight was very cool, and it was very unique and historic, but I also feel like we never got done what we really wanted to get done. That was win. That was the ultimate goal. We never really got that achieved, although in trying to get there, we went four times in a row, and all of a sudden that was kind of special, too."

—Steve Tasker, special teams

"We had guys who were together for a long period of time. We had guys on our team that knew football. I think that was the bottom line. We knew at certain times what we needed to do as a whole team. We did have our scouting department, but I think the guys that I did play with during those four years, they knew a lot of players and they knew their tendencies. They knew things that they struggled at. I think that was the difference for us being the top team in the AFC for four straight years."

—Thurman Thomas, running back

"That's a great experience. It's kind of like a once-in-a-lifetime experience, and being part of the four teams that went to a Super Bowl, you got to experience it four times. That's a feeling you'll never forget for the rest of your life."

—James "J.D." Williams, cornerback

"I think we jelled as a team as far as getting key players in the right positions. Everything just started meshing, and we realized what we had. Everybody just played their position the best they could. It was awesome! When a team comes together like that, it's a good feeling for everybody. If you would have told me I'd have a chance to win four Super Bowls, almost five if we didn't lose to Cincinnati in '88, I would have never thought that anybody on one team could get to four Super Bowls in a row. That's a hard one because you just don't ever think of that. The Super Bowls were a lot more than I expected. Our first one in '90 against the Giants was during Desert Storm. There were a lot of other things out there in the air. We didn't even know if we were going to have a Super Bowl or not have a Super Bowl.

People can say, 'They went to four straight Super Bowls, but they didn't win any of them.' But look at our record. I dare you to find anybody that has a better record than ours in those five years."

—Jeff Wright, nose tackle

chapter 12

In the Trenches

For four consecutive years, Fred Smerlas's seasons ended in the warmth of Honolulu's Aloha Stadium, as he was selected to play in the Pro Bowl from 1980 to 1983.

The (Almost) Natural

The NFL's Dallas Cowboys had one idea. Billy Shaw, an All-America offensive tackle at Georgia Tech where he also played defensive end, had another. And after selecting him in the second round of the 1961 AFL draft, the Bills smartly sided with Shaw.

"[The Cowboys] wanted me to play at linebacker! I never played linebacker before, and I just didn't want to try to play a new position," Shaw said. "The AFL drafted first, and they [Buffalo] drafted me and told me that I would either play defensive end or they would possibly try me on the offensive side of the ball at guard. So I signed with the Bills before the NFL draft because they were going to play me at positions that I was used to playing. But because of the infancy of the AFL at the time, the Cowboys went ahead and drafted me, although I had signed with the Bills, in the anticipation or hopes that the AFL would fold."

While the Cowboys would be incorrect, Shaw showed up at Buffalo's training camp and came across as if he had been playing guard all his life. But in fact, he had only taken up the position a month earlier while practicing for the annual College All-Star Game in Chicago.

"I was playing defensive end and not really doing a good job at it," admitted Shaw. "My nemesis all the way through my career in Buffalo was a defensive tackle in Boston by the name of Houston Antwine. Houston was one of those players that might have been six feet tall, if he stretched. But Houston weighed about 280 and had a really low point of gravity. He was extremely quick and gave me fits. But at the All-Star Game, about halfway through the practice session, Houston was playing offensive guard and not doing a real good job at it. I was playing defensive end and not doing a real good job at it, so Otto Graham, who was our coach, swapped us. That was his salvation and mine as far as football was concerned. When I came to Buffalo, they played me at guard immediately."

Having to wait until his second year before being selected to play in the AFL All-Star Game, Shaw would end the next seven consecutive seasons with the same acknowledgment. Later chosen for the All-Time All-AFL team, in 1999 he was enshrined into the Pro Football Hall of Fame.

"It is certainly an honor that I cherish, but not so much individually. Being the only Hall of Famer to be inducted who played his whole career in the AFL, there was a love affair in the AFL. It was made up of guys that had spent a great deal of time in the NFL, and then there were guys that had shunned the NFL and chose the AFL, which I was a part of. I kind of look at my induction as a person there representing those guys that toiled for so many years in the AFL, mostly in obscurity. It's an honor to represent them."

Dropping the Anchor

Beginning in 1961 and through the next eight seasons, the Bills played 126 regular-season games; 42 preseason games; and four postseason games, including for the 1964, 1965, and 1966 AFL championships. Some games they won, some they lost, and some they even tied. But what was by and large the same regardless of the outcome was that No. 50, Al Bemiller, would be anchoring the offensive line at center. And when he was not there, he was just one step away and playing at guard. What does he attribute that dependability to?

"The big *L*! Luck! A lot of luck," said the modest and humorous Bemiller. "And also I tell people that I always tried to stay away from the big boys [on opposing defensive lines] because I did all the line calls. I'd see big Ernie Ladd sitting off to my left and I was supposed to get him, I'd sic [Billy] Shaw on him. I'd go the opposite direction." All kidding aside, Bemiller proved to be as reliable and as tough as a 10-penny nail. Without question, he had his share of injuries, but pain was not going to sideline the Syracuse alumnus.

"Back then we only had 33 ballplayers. You had to play," Bemiller said. "It wasn't like today where you take a couple days off, a couple weeks off, or a month off. You come back and you get your job back. It wasn't that way. If you got injured, unless you were a superstar, you're gone! So I played through injuries, sure. Not major ones. I was very, very lucky."

That was until the 1969 season finale in San Diego, a 45–6 loss to the Chargers. Bemiller tore a ligament in his knee that required surgery. Still, it was not the injury that put him on the sideline.

"No, I was in very good shape. I came back [for the 1970 season] and there were no problems with my knee. Then [John] Rauch came in [as head coach] and cleaned house," said Bemiller. "Of course, I was in pretty good company. Guys like [Ron] McDole, who later became an all-time great in Washington. And he got rid of [Booker] Edgerson. He got rid of a bunch of us. I could have gone on and played. I was picked up by Detroit, and at the time, I had just opened a nightclub out in Hamburg, and it was going great guns. So I thought, 'No, I'm going to stay here with the club,' and that's what I did.

"Now years and years and years later, you think, 'Jeez, why didn't I go for that?' I had another two, three, four years in me. I know I did. I was very lucky in the sense that my body at that time was very young. It didn't bother me. It got easier for me. The training camps, believe it or not, got easier for me. You know when to run, when to sit, when to take a drink of water, all that kind of stuff. Of course, then you think back, if I would have gone then I could have really got hurt. So I had a great career."

Sturdy as the Rockpile

Defensive tackle Jim Dunaway was Buffalo's second-round draft choice in 1963. He remained on the team for nine seasons before he and wide receiver Marlin Briscoe were traded to Miami in June 1972 for the Dolphins' first-round draft pick the following year and linebacker Dale Farley. But while he wore the Bills uniform, Dunaway, a four-time AFL All-Star, and right defensive tackle Tom Sestak, also a four-time league All-Star, formed the foundation of a rock wall in the middle of the Rockpile.

"I think we had a team that played together very well. When you could depend on the guy next to you, you don't have to worry about him, you have to worry about your job," said Dunaway. "He was probably, to me, the best defensive tackle that I played with. Ever! I admired him because he was older in one sense, but he could get the job done. Really get it done. A lot of times he would not practice all week and would just come play the games because his knees were so bad at the end. He'd come in and play like that, and then he'd go back and have both knees in ice after the game. And lots of operations! You have to give a man a lot of credit for putting that kind of effort into it.

"And I guess it was my second year, '64, the paper said that he 'made a weenie out of Sweeney,' who was the guard for San Diego, and 'putty out of Budde,' from Kansas City, who was a guard for them. He just had such a natural knack for the ball and pass rushing and strength. I just wish his knees hadn't been bad and he could have continued to play. You didn't worry about the right side when he was in there. You knew that the job was going to get done."

Switch!

No question, Ken Jones could have been given the nickname "Switch" during his 11 seasons with the Bills.

An All-America offensive guard at Arkansas State, he was one of the team's second-round draft choices in 1976. But because Pat Toomay had been selected by Tampa Bay in the league's expansion draft, and because of trades—Walt Patulski to St. Louis and Earl Edwards to Cleveland—Buffalo's head coach Lou Saban switched Jones to defense during his first training camp.

"They needed defensive ends and asked if I would switch. I said, 'Sure, no problem.' So they tried me out there for a while, and about halfway through the season, they kind of figured that I should go back over to offense," said Jones, who was credited with 29 tackles, one sack, and two fumble recoveries. "I did start the first eight games my rookie season along with Sherman White, who they got from Cincinnati. And then [that year's third-round draft pick] Benny Williams continued the last part of the season. I did like the defensive side of the ball because it was more aggressive. You kind of were on your own over there. But a lot of guys were telling me that your longevity is better on the offensive side because you're kind of issuing the blocks and you know where you're going to go and how you're going to do it. Unless it's a freak accident, you normally play for a little bit longer over there."

Starting the first two games of 1977 at left tackle for an injured Dave Foley, Jones backed up the veteran for the remainder of the year and became the starter the following season. That's when he made another switch, going from wearing uniform No. 73 to No. 72.

"I switched numbers three times, believe it or not. Sixty-nine was my defensive number. Seventy-three is when I switched to offense," Jones said. "My first season on the offensive line, I had a tendency to hold. And sometimes when you're, I'd say, thrown out to the lions, you have to do what you can do to survive. Sometimes you had to hold. Being a rookie, once you get stapled with that, the refs kind of looked at that and they'd see films from the week before and say, 'Oh yeah, 73 here, we've got to watch him!' Those films go around all over, and they have it written down. Plus, a rookie, they call on those all the time anyway.

"So I think it was around the third game of the season, [Bills head coach Chuck] Knox switched numbers with me and Jonny Borchardt. I took 72, and the next game, I didn't have any holding penalties. I think I had nine in [the previous] three games. It was to the point to where they really were looking at me. Jonny was an offensive guard at the time, and he was sitting on the bench. So either the refs thought that they benched me or else… It worked because I don't think I had but one holding penalty, maybe two, the rest of the season."

Bright Guard

It is an understatement to say that guard Jon Borchardt was a smart player. With his having earned a degree in microbiology at Montana State with a 3.5 grade point average, odds are favorable that he may actually be able to figure out how to put a square peg into a round hole.

During a Monday night game against Miami on October 12, 1981, Borchardt, in his third year as a reserve, stepped in to fill a hole on Buffalo's offensive line after veteran guard Reggie McKenzie suffered a knee injury.

"Reggie got hurt on the fourth or fifth play, so I ended up playing the rest of the game," said Borchardt. "I actually was selected as the Offensive Lineman of the Game by International Harvester. I got a plaque and a couple thousand dollars to give to my favorite charity. So my first almost entire game was a good one. And then I started in New York [the following Sunday versus the Jets], and I think I played okay. I was at left guard, so I was playing against Joe Klecko some of the time, and then they had Abdul Salaam playing there, too."

Borchardt and the Bills were back in the Monday night spotlight on November 9, when they traveled to Dallas with a 6–3 record to take on the 7–2 Cowboys. "Their [defensive] front four was having a great year. Especially Randy White! He was just killing people! He took [star guard Bob] Kuechenberg from Miami and just tore him a new one, weeks before. And even [New England's All-Pro guard] John Hannah had his hands full with him," Borchardt said. "So Chuck [Knox] came up to the offensive linemen at the Wednesday practice and said, 'Come here! Gather up! We don't stand a cut dog's chance in hell of winning this game unless we can handle their front four.' Then he looked at me and said, 'Especially Randy White!' Basically the message was sent. You guys have got a hell of a challenge in front of you!"

Dallas scored 20 points in the third quarter and won the challenge that evening in Texas Stadium, 27–14.

A Hull of a Center

Buffalo's 1986 training camp was in full swing when Kent Hull landed in Fredonia following three seasons with the USFL's New Jersey Generals. The free-agent center chose to sign with the Bills out of nine NFL suitors, and it took all of five days before he was atop the depth chart and starting in the third preseason game.

"I was coming out of the USFL, and I really hadn't proved myself, and I just wanted a chance," Hull said. "I told my wife that I was going somewhere where there was a need for me and not necessarily for the money. Buffalo had Tim Vogler as the starting center, and he injured his knee and was going to be out for six weeks. I said I know I'll get six weeks in, so I picked Buffalo just to show what I could do. It was the best decision I ever made in my life."

Hull and quarterback Jim Kelly became members of the Bills the same day and helped the team become contenders three seasons later by reaching the 1988 AFC Championship Game against Cincinnati. Two seasons after that they were the conference champions for the first of four consecutive years.

"There were a lot of factors, and Coach Levy obviously was the largest factor. I think the prior coaching staff was more of a boot camp–type deal. When Marv came in, it became 'Let's work hard, but let's work smart.' He knew how to treat players," said the three-time Pro Bowl selection. "Instead of bringing a brown bag to the stadium with you, we had lunches served to us. And you weren't scared about being released the next day. I think that's when we became a family and a team. And when you do that, I think you perform like that. The different makeup of every player, when you become a family like that, there are no differences. Marv brought that to us."

Retiring after the 1996 campaign, Hull brought 11 seasons of stability and leadership to the Bills.

"The thing that I'm most proud of is the accomplishments of the people around me. Jim Kelly going into the Hall of Fame. Marv Levy going into the Hall of Fame. I look at the things that Thurman

Free-agent center Kent Hull chose to sign with the Bills out of nine NFL suitors, and it took all of five days before he was atop the depth chart and starting in the third preseason game.

Thomas has done. Andre Reed, James Lofton. I'm proud that I had something to do with what they did," said Hull, a team captain during his final seven seasons. "As an offensive lineman, if you're in the paper, usually it's bad. That's the way it is, and you understand that going into the position. When you pick up that paper on Monday morning after a win, it says, 'Jim Kelly threw for 300-some yards, sacked one time.' Or 'Thurman Thomas rushes for 200-some yards.' That's where most offensive linemen get their gratification. If you look back, it was a very unselfish offensive line. They did not want to be in the spotlight. We got our gratification picking up that paper on Monday and seeing what the people around us did."

Heading Back to Honolulu

For four consecutive years, Fred Smerlas's seasons did not conclude in the cold winter air of Rich Stadium but in the tropical breezes of Honolulu's Aloha Stadium. From 1980 to 1983, the nose tackle was recognized as one of the NFL's best by being selected to play in the Pro Bowl. And following a four-year span, including two seasons when no players from Buffalo were selected (1985 and 1986), in 1988, Smerlas's 10th season, he was named to the AFC's Pro Bowl team for a fifth time.

"When you keep going all the time, you kind of take it for granted. It was kind of like an annual trip," said Smerlas. "You're going to Pro Bowls, and all of a sudden, you're not going! There are several reasons. One is that the coach is not going to push you because he hates you. Things changed. It was so perfect when you get there, and then Chuck [Knox] becomes Kay [Stephenson]. It was very, very difficult. I played poorly. When you rely so much on emotion to play, to just drain yourself, I didn't play well for a couple of years.

"In '84 I didn't play well. In '85 I played okay. And then Braincell [then–head coach Hank Bullough] came in. He kind of rekindled my career because I hated him so much. There was a giant lottery, the state lottery, and I went to the store. Everyone on the team was in line playing the lottery, hoping to win it so they could spit in Hank Bullough's face. Can you imagine that? That's how much we hated him."

Buffalo's second-round draft choice in 1979 continued: "Marv [Levy] came in the second half of '86 and really helped. My hatred toward Hank was so high that when Marv came in, he was anybody but Hank. I was pissed off that I didn't go [to the Pro Bowls], and you start saying to yourself, 'Did I lose it?' So you rekindle yourself. I got fired up and played extremely well. Marv allowed us to have our legs back in games, too, so that helped. We weren't exhausted like we were with Braincell.

"So '88 came, and I made the Pro Bowl, which was just so gratifying. The press said, 'Well, how do you feel? You've been playing great again.' I said, 'No. Not being conceited, but this goes for a lot of the players on the team. Jim Ritcher, Joe Devlin, Darryl Talley, a lot of guys. I've been playing well for a couple years, it's just the [national] press hasn't been here to see it. When you're 2–14, no one sees you. If I'm a New York Giant, I'm in the Pro Bowl 10 times. Because I'm in Buffalo where the media coverage is limited and you're losing, forget about it!

"It was rewarding to go back after the four years because it legitimized the other years, too. Obviously, you must have been playing okay. You don't just resurge after 10 years. You must have been playing at a pretty good level. I started 156 games in a row. So that was really gratifying. It was nice to go back."

Getting His Feet Wet

The highest-drafted offensive lineman in five years, Buffalo's 1990 third-round pick, Glenn Parker, was pressed into service seemingly before he found a set of comfortable shoulder pads in Hojo and Woody's equipment room.

When the season began against the Indianapolis Colts on September 9, nearly 79,000 fans watched from the Rich Stadium seats while fifth-year veteran left tackle Will Wolford watched from the sideline because of a hamstring injury. That meant that Parker would be starting in his first NFL game at the offensive line's spotlight position.

"I had started some of that preseason because he was holding out, so I'd gotten a little bit used to left tackle in the pros," Parker said. "But starting at left tackle in your first game against Duane Bickett was a tough way to get into the league. I did okay. I didn't give up a sack. I gave up a couple of hits on Jim [Kelly], nothing bad. We won the game [26–10]. It was [Colts quarterback] Jeff George's coming-out party, so that's what everybody was talking about, Jeff George getting beat up and crushed. We won, so that's what I remember most. That and just coming through it alive."

After a 13–3 campaign and winning the AFC title, Parker wrapped up his rookie year by playing mostly on special teams in Super Bowl XXV against the New York Giants. The following season, Buffalo posted another 13–3 record and won the AFC championship again. There was one difference, however; in Super Bowl XXVI against Washington, Parker was introduced to the Metrodome crowd in Minneapolis as the starting right guard.

"I'm nervous before every game. That's just typical butterflies and whatnot," said Parker. "But no more nervous than any other game. I was ready to go. Actually, I had a very good game that day. I felt good about our chances. Unfortunately, we just didn't quite get it done."

The Wright Read

When Buffalo hosted Kansas City on January 5, 1992, in its first playoff game of the 1991 season, the offense totaled 448 yards and clobbered the Chiefs, 37–14.

A week later in the AFC Championship Game against the Broncos, the Bills' offense, in a word, struggled. Accumulating 213 total yards, less than half as many as the previous game, they did not find the end zone. On the other hand, Buffalo's defense did.

With the game scoreless in the third quarter and the ball in Denver territory, Broncos quarterback John Elway dropped back and was setting up a screen play to running back Steve Sewell. Buffalo's fourth-year nose tackle Jeff Wright recognized what Elway was attempting to do, stopped the rush, raised his arms, and tipped the pass up into the air. The deflected ball was hauled in by linebacker Carlton Bailey, who then returned it 11 yards for the team's only touchdown. The Bills went on to win, 10–7, and advance to their second consecutive Super Bowl.

"I've had some good coaches along the way, and I'd been taught the game and how many plays you can run out of that backfield set," Wright said. "[Assistant coach] Chuck Dickerson had done an awesome job with our defensive line and schooled us on different formations and how many plays they can run out of that formation. So the recognition of the game, you become one level higher when you get that type of a coach to help you.

"I just read it as soon as I felt the pressure. I backed up and tipped the ball. I didn't try to catch it because I was just watching it and I saw Carlton out of the side of my eye. I thought if we both go for it, one of us is going to drop it. So I just put my hands in the air and moved back from it. I followed him [into the end zone]. That was the difference! That was a huge play! But I wish I would have caught it and been on *Good Morning America* and gotten a little bit higher of a salary sooner."

Don't Ever Give Up

If he discovered change in a pay phone's coin return, Jim Ritcher would likely mail it to the telephone company. An-honest-day's-work-for-an-honest-day's-pay type of guy, he came to Buffalo in 1980 as the team's first-round draft choice and had his work cut out for him despite being a two-time consensus All-America center at North Carolina State and the 1979 Outland Trophy award winner as college football's top lineman. It would be three years before he would get off the Bills' bench and became a fixture at left guard.

Becoming a two-time Pro Bowl selection, Ritcher left the Bills in 1994 after playing 14 seasons and an all-time team record 222 total games, including the four Super Bowls. He never complained about the beginning of his career with the Bills and never bragged about the ending.

"It wasn't something individual as it was just the team," was Ritcher's reply when asked what he is most proud of regarding his Bills career. "Certainly in the first half it was not that the effort wasn't there, but things weren't going right. And just the fact that we didn't give up in the [1993 32-point comeback] Houston wild-card game. I look back on that and there seem to be so many life lessons about not giving up. Showing up and continuing with the work that's before you. Just plug away at it and good things will happen. I try to teach my sons that. Not to ever give up and just keep plugging away.

"I think my career was a little bit like that. I had some success in college, but I got to the Bills and… Here I was a number one draft pick coming in, and I wasn't a starter my first couple years, and I just really felt that I let the scouts and whoever had elected to bring me to the Bills, I really let them down. The people thought enough of me to draft me in the first round and then to not be able to be out on the field, that bothered me."

He continued, "I remember reading an article, and I think the reporter was probably exactly right, but it doesn't mean that it still didn't hurt when I read it. It said, 'Jim Ritcher, is he another first-round flop for the Bills?' I guess we had a number of guys that just didn't pan out previous to me being there. I felt like, gosh, yeah, maybe I am just a flop. So like I said, it was sort of a life lesson to keep plugging away and keep working at it, and things got better.

"We went through a really bad time, back-to-back 2–14 seasons [1984–85], but the team and myself just kept working at it and tried to get better at something every day. Things ended up getting better, and here I finish my career with the Bills by going to four Super Bowls."

chapter 13

The Last Line of Defense

Mark Kelso began wearing his Gazoo helmet, which he is sporting here, in 1989. The helmet was supposed to lessen the risk of concussion.

He Could Go All the Way! Or Maybe Not

In Booker Edgerson's first game, the 1962 season opener against Houston, the cornerback intercepted Oilers quarterback George Blanda twice, as did Marv Matuszak and Carl Taseff in the 28–23 loss. Edgerson would finish the year with six picks for 111 yards and would be named to the AFL's All-Rookie team.

Two seasons later, Edgerson was on the receiving end of another Blanda pass. On November 1, 1964, with a perfect 7–0 record, the Bills hosted Houston, a team that had just two victories. They witnessed an Oilers offensive attack: 93 plays for 428 yards. But coach Sammy Baugh's team came up short and only found the end zone once in the 24–10 game.

Edgerson came up short as well. Late in the fourth quarter, he intercepted Blanda's pass at the Buffalo 1-yard line and returned the ball 91 yards to the Oakland 8. That's right, a 91-yard return. No touchdown.

"I should have run out of bounds in the end zone. I should have kneeled down," laughed Edgerson. "Then they could never say anything about it. It would have just been an interception and that's it.

"Blanda, he threw 68 passes that day. It seemed like 60 of them were to my side. So when I intercepted the ball, I ran it back as best I could. I guess everybody was in pursuit, because I went from one side of the field halfway to the other side, back and forth. And finally, at the 9, [running back] Sid Blanks stepped on my heel and I went down. Everybody said I just pooped out. I said, 'No, no, no.' If you really look at the film close enough you'll see that he stepped on the heel. But nobody accepted that excuse."

The good-natured Edgerson continued. "I was laying on the field and Blanks was laying on the sideline, and Saban said, 'Well, we have to get you in condition.' I raised up and looked over to the sideline, and that's when I saw Blanks. I said, 'What the hell? If he's tired, what makes you think I wouldn't be tired? He's an offensive player. Offensive players are supposed to be in better shape than defensive players."

"Plus, on top of it, I told Lou Saban, 'I got the ball all the way down to the 8, and you guys couldn't even score! You couldn't even get eight yards! You had to kick a field goal, so don't be telling me why I didn't score the touchdown. Why didn't they score the touchdown? They came in fresh!'"

One Move Doubles the Production

Following three seasons as a cornerback and picking off four passes, Tony Greene was moved to free safety by the Bills in 1974, and he more than doubled that interception total with nine pass thefts, even though a knee injury sidelined him for the final two regular-season games and the playoff loss in Pittsburgh.

"I didn't mind [the position switch] at all because at that time we all played bump-and-run up on the receiver and [were] in his face all the time. The receivers, most of the guys were bigger than I was," laughed the 5'10", 170-pound Greene. "So going to free safety, I had full range. I had to tackle a couple fullbacks coming up the middle, but that's all in the game.

"It's a combination of a whole lot of things. You'd like to say you're good and can read offenses, but a lot of interceptions come off of bad throws. You've got to get into the area to make the reception and be quick and fast. I had some good coaching and could read offenses and where plays were going. You just have to give yourself an opportunity to get there."

In addition to becoming Buffalo's starting free safety that year, Greene also became a team captain. What did that mean to him?

"It shows that one, you're responsible. All the guys have faith in you, knowing that you might not be a hothead out there," Greene said. "You're going to try to get everybody up and throw hints out to the defense as far as what might be expected. There's a little pressure on the captain as far as knowing all the defensive coverages that we had."

Pick-Offs Help End the Streak

There is no question that Miami had Buffalo's number during the 1970s. Twenty consecutive games between the AFC East rivals ended with the Dolphins topping the Bills on the scoreboard.

That, however, was not the case when the two teams opened the 1980 season in Rich Stadium on September 7. Buffalo put an end to the streak by winning, 17–7. One of the reasons the Bills came out on top was the play of second-year safety Jeff Nixon. Starting the final five games of his rookie season, Nixon totaled six interceptions for 81 yards, the most picks by a Bills rookie since Butch Byrd snatched seven passes in 1964. In the opener, Nixon collected two interceptions off Bob Griese and one off Don Strock.

"I knew that if there was anything I could do to stop them from continuing that streak, I was going to do it," Nixon said. "It was so nice to see us finally beat them. Not so much for me, but for the older veteran guys that had played for 10 years and had lost every single game. Twenty straight games! It was such a burden lifted from people like Reggie McKenzie and Joe Ferguson and Joe DeLamielleure and all those guys that had been playing for years. And really, that gave us the momentum to really just realize that we were a good team."

Buffalo's and Nixon's momentum continued the following week when another division rival, the New York Jets, visited Orchard Park and left on the short side of a 20–10 final score. Nixon contributed one of Buffalo's touchdowns in the third quarter when he intercepted a Richard Todd pass and returned it 50 yards to the end zone.

"That was interesting. We were in a Cover-2, and with that, both safeties are playing half the field. I noticed they had run a running back out of the backfield, and they really didn't send their wide receivers very deep. They had them on little crossing routes," said Nixon. "So I could really play tight on the running back who was coming up the field, and [Todd] tried to just lob it in there, and I stepped in front of it. At one point I cut back against the grain, and that's what really sprung it for me. That was just a great feeling. That was the only NFL touchdown I ever scored.

"I had this idea of going into the stands, doing the 'Lambeau Leap' or whatever, but instead of doing that, I went to the back of the end zone and I started giving everybody a high-five. I did it with about 30 people. That was a fun moment doing that."

Assuring a Playoff Victory

The combination of experienced coaches, seasoned veterans, talented young players, and unquestionable fan support helped the Bills enter the 1980s with success they had not experienced since the mid-1960s. With an 11–5 record in 1980, Buffalo earned a division title for the first time since 1966.

One of those seasoned veterans, safety Bill Simpson, having played in four NFC Championship Games while with the Rams, knew the mind-set he and his teammates would need to be victorious.

"Once you start to win, everybody starts to get more confidence. I had come from a tradition of winning in L.A. and I think that helped," said Simpson, who signed with Buffalo after five games in 1980. "You just had a real positive attitude when you go out there. You expect to win. That's the mentality that you have to develop, and I think we got that done in Buffalo."

The following season, Simpson helped assure the Bills of their first playoff victory since the 1965 AFL title game when he intercepted Jets quarterback Richard Todd twice in the AFC Wild Card Game. The second pick came with only 10 seconds left in the game. From the Buffalo 11 and trailing 31–27, Todd tried to find receiver Derrick Gaffney in the end zone. His pass found Simpson instead.

"That was a wild game," said Simpson. "We had gone up big, and they were coming back. We were doing a lot of coverages where the safeties had the running back, and we were blitzing a little bit. That specific play, I really had coverage on a back, and the play went away. It was more of a waggle play where backs go one way and the quarterback rolls the other way. I took about four steps and said, 'You know, he's not going to the back. He's coming back to the wide receiver.' I stopped and came back. They were running a little skinny post on the back side, and I just stepped in front of it."

Near-Perfect Attendance

When the Bills played a game from 1975 through 1986, a span of 12 seasons, you knew that No. 22, strong safety Steve Freeman, was more than likely going to be on the field. Buffalo's quiet leader played in 178 out of 179 games. The only one he missed was against Indianapolis on December 2, 1984.

"Three games before I missed the ballgame, we were playing the Patriots and I got hit on the goal line, and it ended up rupturing a thigh muscle. I didn't know it until the next morning. I woke up and couldn't even get out of bed. I couldn't walk. My leg was swelled up about three times its normal size," said Freeman. "I got into the locker room and told Dr. Abe [trainer Eddie Abramoski] that I did something but I don't know what I did.

"We had Dallas the next week, and I was going to play against Dallas if they had to cut my leg off and put a peg up there. So we did all kinds of treatments on it. It was the first time I didn't practice until late in the week. He made me wear a great big ol' giant pad that Earl Campbell wore. I got through the Dallas week and got it hit again right at the end of the ballgame. And then the next week, we played Washington, and I went out and played one play. I got split out with Art Monk. They saw me warming up and knew I couldn't run. They tried an out-and-up on me, and I tackled him and took the pass interference. I came out of the ballgame, and the next week I just couldn't go. We were playing the Colts, and there was no way I could run. I couldn't do anything, so I took a game off. I came back the next week, and it was okay."

If It Helps, Use It!

A studious and calm team leader, Mark Kelso was leading the Bills in interceptions for the third consecutive season in 1989 when the safety added something that a more vain player would not have considered. He began wearing a Gazoo helmet. Nicknamed after the character the Great Gazoo from the television cartoon series *The Flintstones*, it is a protective foam covering that is placed over the actual helmet to help prevent concussions.

"I had a concussion here or there, and then I had a problem with migraines," said Kelso. "After I'd make a hit, it would cause vision problems. It's difficult to play when you're unable to see. You lose your peripheral vision. It becomes a hindrance, certainly, on a football field. And the product was available. I had a great time playing, but it's not something that I wanted to leave the game with a permanent injury or something that I wanted to leave without being able to enjoy the things I wanted to do with my family when I was done playing. It was a postponement of my lifelong career, and I certainly wanted to leave healthy. So it was wear it or don't play. It helped me, and I certainly don't think I would have played much longer without it. It was a great product for me. It prolonged my career. There's no question about it."

Wearing the extra-large helmet for the next five seasons, Kelso, as he demonstrated before the series of concussions, was not afraid to stick his nose in the action. "I had one [a concussion] a few years after that. It [the helmet] didn't prevent everything, but I played with much more confidence after I put it on," said Kelso, who totaled 30 career interceptions and started in Buffalo's four Super Bowl appearances. "It got to the point where when you made a big hit, you'd lose your peripheral vision. And like I said, that becomes a problem. But after I was able to wear that product, I was able to play with that same aggression that I played prior to having those problems."

Finishing the 1992 season with an NFL-coleading eight interceptions and 263 return yards, which ranked fifth all-time in the league's history, Henry Jones was selected to start in the Pro Bowl.

Oh Henry!

Making his first career start in the 1992 season opener against the Los Angeles Rams on September 6, second-year strong safety Henry Jones picked off quarterback Jim Everett twice. He collected two more interceptions two weeks later off Indianapolis's Jack Trudeau, but there was one big difference. Against the Colts, for the first time in team history, both were returned for touchdowns!

Trailing 17–0 midway through the third quarter, Trudeau threw a pass to Rodney Culver that ricocheted off the running back's hands and was grabbed by Jones. One 23-yard return later and the Bills led by 24 points.

"I had flat responsibility, which is the little short area on the outside," said Jones. "He released out for a flat route, and the pass was thrown behind him. He got a finger on it, and I was just breaking on the ball to make a play on him and saw the ball come my way. Everybody was really excited. We had a really good football team, and those types of plays were expected. Everyone was just real professional about it, congratulatory to me."

They were even more congratulatory with a little less than six minutes left in regulation, when Jones swiped another pass and returned it 82 yards to the end zone.

"On that one, we were in a dime situation where I was playing like a linebacker next to Darryl Talley. We both had hook responsibility, and we dropped into the hook area," Jones said. "I think there was a square-in coming in behind me, and just reading the quarterback's eyes, he threw it, I made a break on it, and it hit me right in the chest. I was immediately thinking about scoring. Taking it right up the middle at the linemen and then bending it around the corner and using my speed to head up the sideline. I knew once I got around the linemen, Trudeau was the last guy there because all the receivers had gone deep. I just made a move on Trudeau, gave him a little fake like I was going to cut back on him, and was just gone down the sideline for a touchdown."

With four interceptions and two returns for touchdowns in the first three games, opposing teams may have been better served to look away from Jones. "You know what? I really don't think so," says Buffalo's first-round draft choice in 1991. "I know most teams just usually run their game plan, run the plays that they're comfortable with running against our particular schemes. A lot of times the quarterback wants to challenge you anyway. I know from a defensive standpoint, I want to take on the biggest challenge I can."

Finishing the season with an NFL-coleading eight interceptions and 263 return yards, which ranked fifth all-time in the league's history, Jones's efforts were recognized when he was selected to start in the Pro Bowl.

"I went in one morning with three games left, and I knew the Pro Bowl balloting was coming out. I wasn't really expecting to make it, but I was hoping to. We broke up into offense and defense after the team meeting, and Walt Corey, the defensive coordinator, started calling off names for the Pro Bowl, 'Cornelius Bennett, Bruce Smith, Nate Odomes, and Henry Jones.' I was surprised, ecstatic!"

chapter 14

Called Special for a Reason

Steve Tasker made his mark on special teams during his second season with the Bills, making 20 tackles, forcing three fumbles, and blocking a punt for a safety; he was selected to play in the Pro Bowl that year.

Revenge Is Best Served by Punting

It was not an unfamiliar path for the Bills. Two years earlier, they had claimed quarterback Jack Kemp off San Diego's waivers. And on July 22, 1964, after he had played four seasons with the Chargers, Buffalo picked up linebacker and punter Paul Maguire off their waivers as well.

The event, however, initially left the 1960 first-round draft choice stunned and upset.

"Well, yeah, because my home was there [in San Diego], and I'd started for four years as a linebacker, not just on special teams, and did all the punting," said Maguire. "We had just won the championship in '63, and I got cut the day before training camp. All those guys were great friends of mine. In fact, the day I got cut, most of them were at my house and couldn't understand what the hell had happened.

"It was a shock because we had just bought a new house and my wife was pregnant with our second. Yeah, it was a hell of a shock! It was just one of those deals. When you're with a team long enough, you are either going to get cut or traded. But when you look at what happened after that, why would I even think about being bitter? I was very, very happy. The best thing that ever happened to me was ending up with the Buffalo Bills because we beat San Diego in '64 and '65 in the championship."

Once Maguire was with the Bills, his linebacker days were basically behind him, and he contributed to those two championship teams and the next five seasons as the team's punter.

"I was the fourth linebacker behind [Mike] Stratton and [John] Tracey, the two outside guys, and Harry Jacobs was the middle linebacker. Those guys didn't miss a game in three years! And then we got [Marty] Schottenheimer and a guy by the name of [Bill] Laskey and guys that came in for linebackers," Maguire said. "I ended up just playing all the special teams for seven years. It wasn't one of those deals where I should be playing. I'd like to be playing, yeah, everybody would. But the problem is that I'd already had a chance to play for four years, so it wasn't like I never had a chance to start and play as a linebacker; I did that. So it was very easy."

Gooooooooalgolak!

When in Rome... Scratch that. When in Ogdensburg, New York, and you are a 14-year-old soccer player who recently arrived in the country with your family following the Hungarian revolution, and your new school does not field a soccer team, you kick for the football team. Soccer style.

Pete Gogolak went on to play for Cornell University and was drafted by the Bills in 1964. His first training camp turned teammates into onlookers. Soon, the rest of the AFL and its fans followed suit.

"It was a big thing because nobody had ever kicked the ball sideways," said Gogolak. "They said, 'Where did this guy come from? Everybody's kicking the ball straight-on, and he comes from a 45-degree angle and hits the ball with his instep.' So it was a big novelty all over the league. Every time we played some place they had a big story. Basically, it proved that this type of kicking works."

While that may be true, initially some of Gogolak's teammates needed to be convinced. Particularly the holder.

"[Jack] Kemp was very concerned," said Gogolak. "In practice, this rookie comes in and says, 'Let's try some field goals,' and he saw me lining up from the side and says, 'Hey, Coach Saban! What is this guy doing? I'm not going to hold for him; I've got a finger to protect.' That was a concern, and he didn't hold, so [backup quarterback Daryle] Lamonica became the holder.

"I always liked to bring a fresh guy from the sideline. I'd rather come in as a kicker and a holder rather than somebody who's already playing. The reason is if the quarterback who is playing, and I come in, it's usually when the team doesn't go. I don't want a quarterback who is still thinking of the third-down play that he didn't make. I need total concentration. So Lamonica came in with me, and we made a pretty good team."

"No one had ever held for a soccer-style kicker, but he knew exactly how he wanted the ball," said Lamonica. "He wanted me to tilt the ball on long field goals and hold it straight up and down for 30 yards or less. It was not a problem once we worked out how he wanted it. He was a great kicker. His ball just exploded and got great height. Nobody could jump up and block it. He was a real asset."

Taking a Gamble

The start of Greg Cater's career with the Bills in 1980 was, if nothing else, a whirlwind. A 10th-round draft choice, after surviving training camp and the preseason schedule, five days before the season opened, the rookie punter appeared to have made the team.

However, just four days before the season began, it was a different story when he was placed on waivers. "I had no idea what was going on," said Cater. "I remember Chuck [Knox] brought me in and said it was just a maneuver. He said, 'Greg, what we're going to do is, we're going to waive you. But then, once you clear waivers, we're going to reclaim you. If somebody claims you, then we'll have to give you up. But being a 10th-round draft pick, and this being a year where there's not a great, great need for punters, I don't think you'll be claimed. But it could happen. It takes 24 hours before you clear waivers.'"

Not likely the biggest gamble Knox ever took during his coaching career, but it worked. Cater was not claimed by another team and was back on Buffalo's roster in time for the season opener against Miami and to witness team history. The 17–7 victory ended Buffalo's 10-year, 20-game losing streak against the Dolphins.

"We had talked about it during the week and, of course, discussed the fact that we should have beaten them in the home opener the year before and I guess got beat 9–7, missed a field goal in the last few seconds of the game. So we really felt like this was the year. We had a pretty good football team. I don't really think we knew just exactly how good we were."

In addition to posting the first two punts of what would be his four-year stint with the Bills, Cater also threw the only pass of his career: a 15-yard toss to rookie tight end Mark Brammer.

"The way that thing was drawn up was not the way it actually was run," laughed Cater. "The play was designed for a certain look that we did not get. I remember going, 'This ain't it! This ain't it!' But Jim Haslett was one of the upbacks, and he recognized the look. What he did, rather than running the route he was supposed to run, he took his man across the field, which really cleared the center for Mark. We really had a zone to throw to. It was completed, and we got a first down. And even though we didn't score on it, it seemed to really change the complexion of the game."

Waiver Wire to the Pro Bowl

After taking the field with Houston for two games in 1986, Steve Tasker suffered a knee injury and was placed on the injured reserve list. But after seven weeks, other players getting hurt dictated that the Oilers activate the second-year receiver.

"I was ready to come off of I.R. and was going to play in the slot that week in the three-wide package," said Tasker. "They said, 'We'll put you on waivers on Thursday night, and you'll come off Friday night.' So I said, 'What's that mean?' They said, 'Well, it's really nothing. It's just a procedural thing that we have to do.' So they did it, and when the 24 hours was up, we were notified that there was a team that claimed me. It was Buffalo!" Tasker was claimed by the Bills just two days before they hosted Pittsburgh on November 9, in what would be the first game for a new head coach named Marv Levy.

"I found out on Friday night that I'd just been picked up, and then Saturday morning at 5:00 AM, I got on a flight to Buffalo," said Tasker. "I got there midmorning and went over to the stadium and got my physical. I actually flunked, and they decided they would take a chance and whatever happened, they would take responsibility for. That night, I was introduced to the team by Marv, and the next day I suited up and went out on the field."

Buffalo won that game, 16–12, to improve its record to 3–7 and finished with a 4–12 mark. The team played better under Levy during the following strike-shortened season, and Tasker did not have to worry about seeing his name back on the waiver wire. Making his mark on special teams, he made 20 tackles, forced three fumbles, blocked a punt for a safety, and was selected to play in the Pro Bowl.

"We were in a team meeting, and I was just kind of sitting there, and [assistant coach] Walt Corey walked over and shook my hand. It was kind of weird because guys usually don't come into the team meeting and shake hands," laughed Tasker. "He shook my hand and looked down and smiled at me and whispered real soft, 'You made the Pro Bowl.' Every player, especially a guy like me playing special teams, wants to be accepted as a real player, wants to be thought of as a player that other guys would know and vote for. I'd never really experienced a happier moment in the NFL than that. There were happier moments for the team, but for me, personally, I think that was it."

A Special Special-Teams Star

In 1987 Buffalo drafted Shane Conlan and traded for Cornelius Bennett. That linebacker windfall prompted Mark Pike, who had been on the injured reserve list the previous season as a rookie because of hamstring and foot injuries, to be moved to defensive end, the position that he played at Georgia Tech.

A fine defensive lineman? Certainly. But Pike's main contribution to the Bills would be on special teams, where he would prove to be sensational.

"It all kind of worked out really well. I got back to a position that I was a little more familiar with," said Pike. "Ted Cottrell was my defensive line coach that year, and I think he saw a lot of the same things that they saw in me at linebacker. I was just a guy who worked hard. I could run well and had a lot of potential. And then, of course, on special teams that first year, I made some big hits and some big plays and kind of captured the eye of Marv [Levy] and Coach [Bruce] DeHaven. In a lot of ways, Steve Tasker had some similar plays in his career early that did the same thing for him. It kind of catapulted him into where people really talked about him, and coaches talked about him as being an outstanding player."

The combination of Pike and Tasker proved to be an outstanding special teams duo—arguably the best one-two punch in the NFL! "I realized early that that was my meal ticket. I realized that I had to be a good position player or I wouldn't be around. I think Steve did, too," Pike said. "I don't want to say we didn't focus on our positions, but we put the extra focus to our special teams. Making that as important as playing offense or defense. We prepared that way, we studied film that way, and we practiced that way. Me and Steve became the two leaders of the special teams for years because of that.

"Later in my career, half the time I felt like I was a coach. Your coaches can coach you so much, but then the younger players, they like to talk to players who have been there and been through it. We just took it more seriously than a lot of players do. We took it to the next level. I played special teams at a time when the importances of special teams were really evolving in the league, and obviously, Steve did too. We were, I don't want to say pioneers, but we were two guys that really were there and were really good performers when the special teams was really becoming big in the league and the importance was becoming universal among all the teams.

"Of course, Marv was a real important part of that, too. That's how his roots had started. He kept players around like Steve and myself and some of the long-snappers that we had, because he knew how important it was. You have a lot of young guys that normally play on special teams, so I think he looked at me as a guy that's a great on-the-field leader, a guy that can solidify these teams each year."

Christie's Big Boot

Opening the 1993 campaign with back-to-back victories, the three-time defending AFC champion Bills hosted the Miami Dolphins on September 26. Having converted all four attempts during the young season, Buffalo's second-year kicker Steve Christie was as perfect as the team's record when he trotted out and booted a team-record 59-yard field goal as time expired in the first half.

Steve Christie, here kicking on January 8, 2000, booted a team-record 59-yard field goal as time expired in the first half against the Miami Dolphins on September 26, 1993.

"It was toward the locker room, and the wind was blowing a little bit behind me and to my left, and it was raining a little bit," said Christie, who signed as a Plan B free agent in 1992. "Marv probably wouldn't call that during the regular part of a game, but because it's the last play of the half, it's one of those deals where, hey, you know what? If you get it, you get three; if you don't, fine. We're not going to get penalized. So it was a 'swing your leg and see what you can do' sort of thing. When you line up for something like that, you know you've got to give it what you have. The biggest thing is getting it over the line first and then getting it over the crossbar at the other end. It's always a good lift to get a big kick like that before the half because you go into the locker room up on a bit of a high, and you've given your team some points on the board to go in with."

Christie's field goal, which would be the longest in the league that year and the fourth-longest in NFL history, was not enough. The Bills lost, 22–13. He did, however, make game-winning field goals in four of Buffalo's 12 victories that season.

"Your goal as a professional athlete, it's not always the big plays, it's just being consistent and being available when you're called on, especially for a kicker. It's an odd job. You really want to be steady and reliable. The 59-yard field goal, that's really not your job. It's only a little part of it. And quite frankly, you're not really expected to make that all the time, but you are expected to make so many from inside the 40 and inside the 30. It's good to know that your team has confidence in you and that you're contributing. That was important for me, to be able to contribute. And the best way to do that is to cap off a game with the game winner."

Mohr Hang Time

On September 13, 1992, Chris Mohr helped set an NFL record without stepping foot onto the field. The Bills and 49ers met in San Francisco, and for the first time, no punts were attempted by either team. "I do recall on the plane ride back home, walking back and telling Chris he wasn't going to get a paycheck that week," laughed Buffalo's head coach Marv Levy.

Four years later in 1996, Mohr set an all-time team season mark by attempting 101 punts. But he did well with the extra work by averaging 41.5 yards per punt, about one yard above his 10-year Buffalo career average.

In a game against Indianapolis on October 6, Mohr punted a career-high 11 times. Five were fair-caught, and two others were not returned. One that was handled resulted in a three-yard loss.

"That's my goal, to have every ball I punt fair-caught or not returned," said Mohr, who signed as a free agent in 1991. "If I'm giving that guy a chance to return the ball, that's giving their team a chance to win. I'm not really doing my job to the fullest if I give them a chance to win. We try to have a goal of net punting 37 [yards]. We try to kick the opponent into trouble at least once per game; that's inside the 10. We try not to have big returns. Other than that big return against the Giants [Amani Toomer's 87-yard return for a touchdown in the season opener], we're doing a good job.

"It's great to be on a team that really cares about the special-ists and the special teams. That's something that goes a long way with me. Being on a team where you're appreciated and get along well with all the guys, it makes a big difference, and it shows in our performance."

chapter 15

I.R.

Following an All-Pro season, in which he had a league-leading 17.5 sacks and 126 tackles and earned the NFL's Most Valuable Player award, Bryce Paup suffered a groin injury three games into the 1996 season that caused him significant trouble and led to him sitting out four of the final six games.

Talked Out of Retirement

During the Bills' first three years of existence, running back Wray Carlton totaled 1,374 yards, averaging 4.1 yards per carry, and scored 13 touchdowns. He found the end zone four more times on receptions. In 1963, however, an injury did what many opponents had difficulty doing. It stopped him.

"That was a hard time for me. I had a really bad groin injury. I dressed for four games and played in two. It was so bad that they sent me home. They said, 'You're done. You're not going to heal for a while,'" said Carlton.

"I was really discouraged, and I considered retirement. I wrote a letter to the Bills and to [general manager] Dick Gallagher in particular, and said, 'I'm not really healing up that well. I don't think I can play anymore. I really don't want to play.' So he announced my retirement, and I was all done. But then I got a call from Jack Kemp, and he said, 'What are you doing? You can't quit now. You're only 25 years old!' I said, 'Well, I'm not sure that I want to play anymore.' He said, 'You've got to come back. We're on the verge here of something really good. With you back, I think we can do something and maybe even win the championship.' So I was thinking about it, and Ralph [Wilson] called, and so I decided to come back.

"When I got back in '64, in training camp, I got hurt again. I broke three ribs in a game. I was on the shelf for the first three or four games, and the team was really doing well. So [Lou] Saban said, 'We're on a roll. Can you sit and wait?' And so I kind of waited around until there were maybe three games left in the year. We started to stall out a little bit toward the end there, and Saban called me into his office and said, 'Are you ready? I think we need you in there. We need your blocking and your power running because of the weather. It's getting cold. I'm going to activate you.' So he activated me for the last three games, and we went on to beat San Diego [in the AFL Championship Game]."

Duby's Streak Is Stopped

Elbert "Golden Wheels" Dubenion was like a mailman. The outstanding wide receiver delivered in sun, rain, sleet, or snow during Buffalo's first four years. But on September 26, 1965, three games into the season, his streak of 75 regular- and postseason games came to a close. Hosting the Jets, the Bills led 13–10 in the third quarter when Jack Kemp connected with Dubenion on an 11-yard pass in the end zone. The ball and New York's defensive back Willie West arrived roughly at the same time. Dubenion held on for the touchdown, but he tore a ligament in his left knee.

"The knee caught the ground and flopped off in a direction, and that's when I got a little concerned. It went outward instead of inward," Dubenion said. "Billy Shaw beat everybody there and knocked the people away from me. Then Dr. [Joseph] Godfrey told me to meet him at Buffalo General [Hospital] in the morning. It was everything. MCL. Dr. Godfrey said it was bad, but he fixed it up."

With Dubenion still in the hospital a week later when the Bills met the Oakland Raiders at War Memorial Stadium, Buffalo got the 17–12 victory, and he got company. "Glenn Bass, the other receiver, got hurt, and they brought him into Buffalo General. I heard somebody moaning, and so I got my crutches and went in there and said, 'What's the matter, Glenn?' He said, 'I can't play.' I said, 'Are they still paying you?' I thought he heard they weren't going to pay him," laughed Dubenion. "We didn't do this on purpose; I know I didn't. I thought he had bad news or something by crying, 'I can't play.' I said, 'Do the best with what you've got. We didn't do this on purpose. Relax.'"

An Unfortunate Part of the Game

Like interceptions, fumbles, and missed field goals, injuries are unfortunately a part of the game of football. In 1974 Buffalo's second-year outside linebacker John Skorupan was building on his first-season performance when he was named to the UPI

All-Rookie team, by helping the Bills post wins in four of their first five games. He and his teammates hoped to make it five out of six when the New England Patriots visited Orchard Park on October 20. What Skorupan didn't seek was a season-ending knee injury.

"Just a pileup; I think [running back] Sam Cunningham walked on me, and it just popped out," says Skorupan, a 1973 sixth-round draft choice from Penn State. "It wasn't a major blow or anything like that. The ligaments popped a little bit. I don't think it would have required an operation nowadays. The technology wasn't there for the scoping and everything. But it was pretty disappointing because we went to the playoffs that year in [my hometown of] Pittsburgh, and I didn't get a chance to play."

So instead of being alongside his teammates as they compiled a second consecutive 9–5 record and made the postseason for the first time since the 1966 AFL Championship Game, Skorupan spent the fall and winter months recuperating and rehabilitating his right knee.

"It was tough. That was the first time I'd ever been seriously injured. Major surgery and then you're in a cast for six weeks. I had skinny legs before I was in a cast. Afterward, I had a lot skinnier legs," laughed Skorupan. "It was just an uncertainty and not knowing. And quite honestly, through my career, I had a second knee operation, and the thing I'm most proud about is being able to come back from two surgeries and still being able to play. Because it's a hard rehab! It takes a lot of work and determination to come back from major surgery like that."

Tackled by Hepatitis

Roland Hooks arrived at Buffalo's training camp in 1975 coming off a productive senior season at North Carolina State, rushing for 850 yards, a 6.3-yards-per-carry average, and finding the end zone 18 times. Still, trying to make a team whose leading running back was just two years removed from setting an NFL rushing record can be intimidating. The challenge becomes even greater when the team's medical staff unexpectedly sends you home.

"I went to the rookies training camp and took the physical. I was catching a bus to go back to the hotel and it might have been Abe [head trainer Eddie Abramoski] who pulled me aside and said I had hepatitis, and I had to go home until it cleared up," said Hooks. "I was pretty shocked. I didn't know how I contracted it or how it would affect my health. I went home for about four weeks. I was pretty nervous about my chances of getting to play.

"When I came back, there were two preseason games left. I played in the last preseason game [against Kansas City]. I ran a kickoff back 80 yards, so they stuck me in at halfback toward the end of the game. I went out and caught a pass, and someone fell across my ankle and stretched the tendons. And so I had to be put in a cast. They say it was hepatitis that caused me not to play my rookie year, but more likely, it was my injured ankle."

Hooks returned the following season already ahead of the game for two reasons. One, he was healthy. And two, since he had been on injured reserve and ineligible to take the field, he had much more time to learn the Bills' playbook from cover to cover. "I was a lot more comfortable because I had a good idea of the system, a lot more at ease my second year," Hooks said. "I knew the other players and the coaches, and I thought I had enough talent to play in the league based on what I had seen the year before."

Stopped While on Top

Acknowledged as one if the game's premier cornerbacks after being named All-NFL in 1973 and 1974, Robert James appeared to have a future as promising as his immediate past. And having missed only one game through his first six seasons with the Bills, James's reliability was not even so much as a passing thought in the minds of his coaches, teammates, and fans.

That, however, quickly changed during the third preseason game on August 23, 1975, when James suffered what would be a career-ending knee injury against the Los Angeles Rams.

"Jim Harris threw a long pass to Harold Jackson, and I intercepted the ball. I was running it back and really was just trying to score. I should have just gone ahead and fell down, slid down like quarterbacks do today," said James. "I was pushed, and I started stumbling, and I tried to regain my balance, and in the process of trying to regain my balance, [running back] Lawrence McCutcheon hit me on the outside of my right knee and tore all the ligaments. That blow ended my career."

But not without a fight! Although unable to play, James remained with Buffalo for nearly two years before he was waived by the team 10 days into the 1977 training camp. "I really felt like I could come back. Just to show you how bad I wanted to get back, I had three other knee operations just to try to straighten the situation out that I was dealing with. But I was not successful. I told some of the best doctors in the country to just go ahead and operate on my knee, but it just wasn't there. It wasn't in it for me to get full range of motion and flexibility back where I could get back into the game.

"I really loved the game, really wanted to play the game. I felt like if I could have got back, I could have played 16, 17, 18 years. It was something I felt like I was able to do. At the level I was at, I did not see myself regressing. I saw myself progressing. When I got hurt, I still don't think I was at my peak. I think I was still on the incline, so this is why I really, really wanted to get back to see what I truly could accomplish. But once again, it just was not there. I appreciate and I thank God for the years that he blessed me with, and I thank God for the opportunity that he presented to me, allowing me to even get in to play for as long as I did."

Bad Luck for Nixon

During the first four games of the 1980 season, second-year free safety Jeff Nixon collected five interceptions and helped the Bills post a perfect record. On the first weekend of October, they traveled to San Diego to meet the also-undefeated Chargers. Buffalo won, 26–24, but lost Nixon for the following nine games due to an injured left knee.

"My parents had driven from Phoenix to watch the game. It would be the first game that they'd ever seen me play," said Nixon. "The Bills had made me the honorary captain for the game because I was leading the NFL in interceptions at the time. Then I went out there and got hurt the very first quarter. It was a real depressing moment for me."

Unfortunately for Nixon, he would experience another depressing moment during the Bills' 1981 training camp.

"I got there, and I thought everything was going good, and they had us doing a dummy drill, where you're tackling a dummy. I went driving into it, and when I planted my left knee, it gave out on me. They didn't put me on injured reserve because they wanted to see if they could bring me back that year, which they did. I ended up coming back and playing some games.

"That was the beginning of a tough period for me as far as football. I knew there was something wrong with my knee, but I figured, 'Hey, the doctors know what's best for me.' And so every time I'd injure it, they might take out a little piece of cartilage or fix it up a little bit with a brace or something. But after I hurt it again and again and again, they finally decided to do reconstruction surgery. I had five surgeries altogether. They were all arthroscopic except for the total reconstruction. They had to give me the 10-inch zippers on each side of my knee," laughed Nixon. "I think God has a hand in everything, and with that I knew it was just something that I had to go through. Injuries are a part of football. Of course, you don't think about it when you're a healthy person. You don't think, 'Hey, I'm going to get injured.' You just play. But unfortunately this happens to a lot of people in the NFL."

Sidelined by Guillain-Barré Syndrome

Following three seasons as a tailback at Penn State, Booker Moore moved to fullback as a senior and produced 707 yards on 120 carries, a 5.9-yard average. His last collegiate carry was a 37-yard touchdown run late in the Nittany Lions' victory over Ohio State in the 1980 Fiesta Bowl.

Aside from playing in two college All-Star Games, Moore, who was drafted in the first round of the 1981 NFL draft by Buffalo, would not carry the football again until the 1982 season. It all began when he started to feel lethargic while practicing for the Japan Bowl and noticed a decrease in body strength.

"Toward the end of the trip, I was sleeping a lot, but I didn't think nothing of it," said Moore. "When I came back and started working out and was lifting weights, gradually, I couldn't lift as much."

Moore explained what occurred over the next few months. "I think I was benching about 350 pounds and gradually I could barely get 335 up. And then I couldn't do 300. Couldn't do 250. When I got down to about 200, I knew that something was wrong. I went to my personal doctor, went to another regular doctor and to another doctor, and then finally, they sent me to a specialist, a neurologist, and he diagnosed it right away." The neurologist told the Flint, Michigan, native that he had developed Guillain-Barré syndrome, a type of nerve inflammation involving progressive muscle weakness or paralysis.

"First of all, I was relieved to find out. And then the second thing was I didn't know what was going to happen. I'd waited my whole life to get to the NFL and now I'm sick. Is my body going to recover and fight this off? Am I going to get back healthy, first? And then secondly, will I be able to play ball again? There's really no cure. Your body has to fight it off."

Moore fought like a heavyweight champion, but he still had to accept being sidelined during what should have been his rookie season. It was not an easy task. "I think it was harder for me to be there and be around it," he said. "I could learn the plays and learn some of the mental part of playing pro football. It was good for me to be there, but it made it extremely hard to not be able to contribute. That was very, very hard to take. I think looking back, if I would have just removed myself from it and just worked out somewhere and tried to get back healthy, my mental state would have been a lot better. It was a very trying period, but I think it made me a better person and ultimately a better player."

Cleared to play in 1982, Moore was more than just a little excited to finally don a Bills uniform. "It was great in that I worked really hard to build my strength and speed back up. I finally got back and got clearance to play, and then it felt like, now I can start fulfilling my dream. I dreamed about playing pro ball probably my whole life."

Wrong Place at the Wrong Time

There was at least one thing for certain from September 18, 1977, through November 1, 1981. When the Bills took the field, Shane Nelson would be a starting linebacker. That's a span of 72 consecutive games!

Leading the team in 1979 with an incredible 192 tackles, Nelson continued to make stops the following season with 126 tackles, 74 solo. And he would remain in the center of the action until the ninth game of the 1981 season against Cleveland.

"I was doing an inside blitz on [guard] Joe DeLamielleure, who used to be with the Bills, and as I faked him outside and started to come underneath, I had it [my leg] planted. What they did was an illegal chop block. Of course, they wouldn't call it," Nelson laughed. "They set Freddy [Smerlas] up, and they really chopped him over, and all three of them came down on my right knee. I just ended up caught in a pile."

In the wrong place at the wrong time, Nelson, a rookie free agent in 1977, missed the next five games before trying a comeback against New England on December 13. That came to a halt when he reinjured the knee and was sidelined for the season finale at Miami.

After an exhausting rehabilitation that lasted through the following year's training camp, Nelson removed himself from the 1982 season opener against Kansas City when his knee failed him and required surgery. Not one to give less than 100 percent, Nelson was forced to hang up his helmet and shoulder pads.

"That was real difficult because I'd always been a leader on every team I played on," said Nelson. "It's a tough row when you're not able to be out on the field. I think one of the great fundamentals of leadership is leading by example. Which is how you play the game, how you approach the game, how you studied the game. So it [being unable to play] was kind of a comfort-zone issue for me because it was a place I'd never been in.

"As far as being on the sideline and still assuming some leadership of the team, when my knee wasn't ready, I retired rather than just hang[ing] around. I always approached the game with everything that I had, trying to be the best I could, trying to be a team leader. So trying to become a leader from the sideline was not something that I was comfortable with. It was difficult."

Welcome Back, Butler

Even though they were on the wrong side of a 14–9 final score, Buffalo's 1985 season opener against San Diego meant so much to so many. It was the NFL debut of defensive end Bruce Smith, receiver Andre Reed, and kicker Scott Norwood. It was the Bills' debut of quarterback Vince Ferragamo. And it marked the return of All-Pro wide receiver Jerry Butler.

Out of action since suffering a knee injury requiring surgery midway through the 1983 campaign, Butler had to rehab his body and his soul in order to get back on the field. "People that are trying to work back from an injury, it's a mind game. It's very tough not really feeling a part of the team. Every day, I was my own cheerleader. I had so much self-talk of what you had to do and your day and time will come. It was a process of going through a tunnel," said Butler. "That went for a while in '84. All I could think about in the off-season when I was working was, 'I've got to do this!' I was prayerful, and I told God, 'Here's the deal. If I'm able to come back through this, then I have to do something special in return.' I made that vow.

"In training camp down in Fredonia, I struggled here and there, and I was the third-, fourth-string receiver. I was wondering, did this team see value in me? Would they wait for me? By then, Kay Stephenson had taken over [as head coach]. I think Kay was hoping that I would come back. He was pulling for me when he was the [offensive] coordinator under Chuck Knox.

"Our last preseason game, I wound up playing in the fourth quarter, and it dawned on me. Man, I go from a starter in the NFL, a Pro Bowl player, and now I'm playing in the fourth quarter of a preseason game! That doesn't look good. As I moved toward the season, I'm not even sure if I'm going to make the team. I went and made the team, and through that [season-opening] week not being the starter. It got down to Sunday morning right before the game. Kay Stephenson came over to me and said, 'How do you feel?' I said, 'I'm fine.' He said, 'Good. You're starting today.' I thought he was kidding! I didn't prepare myself mentally. I guess I was beating myself up because of how far I had dropped. At that moment in time, I kind of took to myself and just started talking to God and thanking him and [thinking] 'Don't let me go out there and embarrass myself and him at the same time.' I think I had 100-some yards [game-high 140 yards on four catches], and I just had a ball."

Learning While Injured

Philadelphia's loss became Buffalo's gain in 1986. Free-agent safety Mark Kelso was an Eagles late-round draft pick out of William and Mary the previous year, but he was waived during the preseason. The Bills offered a second chance to play in the league and signed him as a free agent.

"I figured I might have an opportunity to play somewhere, and the Bills called. I grew up in Pittsburgh, so it was close to home," said Kelso. "Bill Polian was the player personnel director then, and I had a good feeling about Bill and the direction they were taking. They had good, young guys, and they had some guys that had played for a lot of years. They were starting to turn over and bring in a lot of young guys, so I thought it'd be a good opportunity and a place to play."

After making the roster and playing mostly on special teams, Kelso suffered a left-knee injury during a game against St. Louis on September 21, the third game of the year and Buffalo's first victory, and was placed on the injured reserve list for the rest of the season. He used the time to rehabilitate the injury and learn more about life in the NFL.

"It helped me mature as a player. I loved the game as it was, and I was a student of the game," Kelso said. "I analyzed a lot of film that year, and Coach [Dick] Moseley, who was the defensive back coach, we did a lot of film work for him and spent hours and hours [watching film] when we weren't practicing. That gave me a real feel for what was going on, and I got a chance to watch [veteran safety] Steve Freeman play. He was such a terrific player. I learned an awful lot from him. I understood what my role needed to be and what my responsibilities needed to be."

Becoming a starter the following season, Kelso co-led the AFC with six interceptions. In 1988 he had seven interceptions for a career-high 180 return yards. And in 1989 he led the Bills and was tied for fourth in the NFL with six interceptions. Kelso credits the film work he began as an injured rookie and continued as a veteran as the main reason he accumulated the 19 interceptions during those three seasons.

"No question, you feel more comfortable the more prepared you are. If you feel like there's not anything that's going to surprise you, then you have a real ease about it and you're in a real comfort zone. I had a lot of studying and was able to look at the examples of some of those other people like Steve Freeman and some guys that were playing at that time, and see their work ethic, how they went about their job. And I was able to kind of mimic that performance, that criteria that they used. That enabled me to have some good success."

Breaking Waves and a Knee

Linebacker Eugene Marve was Buffalo's man in the middle for five seasons beginning in 1982, leading the team in tackles three times and finishing second twice. But while he was successful breaking blocks and bringing down ball carriers, he didn't fare as well breaking waves prior to his sixth season in 1987.

"Unfortunately, I was waterskiing on the Niagara River, upstream in Canada, and I busted up my knee. So I went into training camp hurt."

Playing in five nonstrike games, Marve's season came to a close when he dislocated an elbow against the Broncos on November 8. That also brought an end to his Bills career. Traded to the Buccaneers for a draft choice during the following offseason, Marve did not exactly leave for Tampa with a smile on his face.

"Walt Corey came from Kansas City [to become the defensive coordinator that season], and when he came, he brought in two or three linebackers with him," Marve said. "So he favored those linebackers and, of course, the opportunity was there for them to play because I was hurt. It was my sixth year, and it was a different time in my football career. In my 10 years of playing, four in college and six in the pros, I had always been one of the coach's favorite. I had never been hurt and sidelined.

"I think I really handled the situation with Walt Corey in a very immature way, in the sense that I disenfranchised myself with him. I thought he was showing his guys favoritism. Me and him didn't speak very much that year. It was a situation where I wish I could have really handled myself as more of a veteran-type player. But I couldn't play because I was hurt. I had what I called the 'pressure cooker' back when I was playing. And that's what I felt I was under, a pressure cooker!

"As I matured out of that situation in Tampa, I realized that I could only put myself in a pressure cooker. I think the organization, Walt Corey, had decided that they were going to go in the direction of the new linebackers that they had. And Walt Corey's first year was '87, so he had no loyalty toward me and knew [little] of my abilities of playing football. Buffalo was a great place for a young man to mature. Not only financially, but as a man. Buffalo will always hold a special place in my heart."

Why Me?

It is unfortunate, but true. Football is a physically brutal game, and the conclusion of a player's career can occur on any play. No one knows that better than Derrick Burroughs. During the second quarter of a September 24, 1989, game in Houston's Astrodome, Buffalo's fifth-year cornerback was covering Oilers wide receiver Curtis Duncan on a routine play that did not have a routine ending. For Burroughs and his teammates, in fact, it was frightening.

"I got into a jaw-jacking contest with Duncan, and he caught a slant, and I should have actually pulled off, but I was trying to get more of a tackle on him than I probably should have, and I ducked my head a little bit too low," Burroughs said. "Along with me ducking my head, I got a hit in the back, so it kind of compressed my spinal cord, which caused a temporary paralysis from my neck down.

"I know that I'm a blessed guy, because I'm probably one of the few people in America that knows what it's like to walk and knows what it's like to be paralyzed from the neck down and then to walk again. That's the scary thing, to know what it's like to be a quadriplegic. I never want to experience that again."

Burroughs, who along with defensive end Bruce Smith was chosen in the first round of the 1985 draft by the Bills, was immediately immobilized on the field and had the paralysis for approximately an hour. During and after the recovery, rehabilitation, and ultimately, retirement, he admits a question did cross his mind: why me?

"I never missed going to church regardless of the way I acted sometimes on the field," said Burroughs, who had been ejected from the 1988 AFC Championship Game loss in Cincinnati after

Derrick Burroughs experienced a temporary paralysis from his neck down after a hit to the back compressed his spinal cord in 1989.

throwing a forearm to Bengals receiver Tim McGee's face mask and arguing with officials. "I don't smoke. I don't drink. I don't do drugs. I always try to live my life pretty decent. I tried to live the right way.

"Then I started growing older and getting a little more in touch with the man upstairs and understanding that the same guy that gave you everything has the right to take anything away that he wants to. So as I got older, and as I understood it better, I stopped questioning it because I'm walking. That's the prize of the whole thing: I'm walking. Being a part of the NFL is great. Being a pro football player is wonderful. But being able to walk is more important than anything in the world. When I understood that, I stopped asking why."

Face to Face with Rehab

How did John Davis become the starting right offensive guard in 1990? Hard work. Nothing more, nothing less. The following season, however, he faced a potentially career-ending knee injury and would have to work even harder if he was to step back on the field again.

Buffalo began its defense of the 1990 AFC championship with 10 victories out of 11 games before heading to Foxborough, Massachusetts, on November 24, 1991, to meet the Patriots. While the Bills lost the game, 16–13, they also lost Davis after he caught a cleat in the muddy field during a field-goal attempt and a New England defender fell on him, blowing out Davis's knee.

"It was very frustrating simply because I felt like that was by far my best season that I was playing," said Davis, who had signed with Buffalo as a Plan B free agent in 1989. "I felt that my '90 season was good, but I felt that my '91 season, I had just taken another step and had played consistently well the whole year as far as grading out, no penalties, and no sacks."

The injury forced Davis to undergo season-ending major reconstructive surgery. He would wear a cast and face strenuous rehabilitation while his teammates faced the rest of the schedule and, ultimately, a trip back to the Super Bowl.

"The toughest part was knowing I wouldn't get to play. And you're not part of the team, regardless of what people say. You're rehabbing, and as much as you want to play, and as much as your teammates want you to play, you're not in the everyday activities of the team. I give a lot of credit to Mr. Abe [Eddie Abramoski], the trainer at the time, and to [assistant trainer] Bud Carpenter. They did a wonderful job. It was hard on all of us because we all knew how much I wanted to get in and play. But you have to be smart about it."

The Georgia Tech alumnus was Einstein-like and achieved his personal goal of returning in one year. Missing 13 games, including Super Bowl XXVI, Davis stepped back onto the Rich Stadium turf on December 6, 1992, against the Jets and played on the field-goal unit, the same position he was playing when the injury occurred.

"I had asked the coaches [about that]. I said, 'Look, I don't want to go back in on that team until I am 100 percent confident that nothing's going to happen or that I'm strong enough.' And that's the first thing I went out on the field for!" Davis said. "So a lot of emotions were running through me. I didn't want to be out there, but I did want to be out there. It gave me a good opportunity to get my feet wet again in an actual game situation. I started gaining a little bit more confidence each week. If you look at it now, I wasn't ready to play. I thought I was at the time, but I wasn't. But you know what? The opportunities come few and far between to play in the NFL, and I was going to do anything I could possibly do to get back on that field.

"I worked my way in and would spell Glenn Parker a little bit. And then to know that I did get to play in the Los Angeles Super Bowl [XXVII versus Dallas].... Then finally the next year, I started three games at center because Kent Hull was hurt. It was still up in the air whether I was going to start at guard or not because Glenn had been playing so well and we were still competing. I eventually got the opportunity to start. And then coming back and practicing [for Super Bowl XXVIII] at Georgia Tech; I grew up an hour from Atlanta and playing in the Georgia Dome was by far the most special time. Our son was fixing to be born, so there was a lot of stuff on the outside that made that Super Bowl nice."

The Only Way He'd Slow Down

Although injuries are a part of the game, the timing could not have been much worse for linebacker Bryce Paup. Following an All-Pro season in which he had a league-leading 17.5 sacks and 126 tackles and earned the NFL's Defensive Most Valuable Player award, Paup suffered a groin injury three games into the 1996 season that would trouble him for the rest of the year. In fact, it became so painful that Paup would sit out four of the final six games.

"It wasn't completely debilitating where I couldn't play," said Paup, who had 11.5 fewer sacks and 52 fewer tackles than the previous season. "But slowly, it pared out things that I could do in my game. I had to just slowly take things out that I couldn't do anymore because of the pain. No matter what I tried doing, it didn't get any better. Eventually it did tear somewhat. It never completely tore off the bone, but the MRI showed a defect there. I went to see some specialists, and they saw some things that were typical in that kind of an injury.

"Before that, I don't think anyone ever considered a groin injury a major injury. To me I knew it was because there wasn't anything I could do. And I think a lot of people on the team actually questioned me and what I was doing or maybe what I wasn't doing. That was the hardest part, I think, to have teammates making little comments about if I was going to be back, on the field or whatever. It was just to the point where I couldn't. That was the worst part for me.

"They were joking, but to me, there's a little bit of truth in jokes. They're getting somewhere where they're not willing to come out and actually say it, but they're getting to the point through a joke or through some snide comment. For me, I never had to deal with that [before] because I could always play through something. It got to the point where I just couldn't go anymore, and there was nothing I could do about it. It took a whole off-season and halfway through the next season for it to completely go away. So that was the most frustrating injury and longest injury that I had ever had."

"If I'm Walking, I Can Play"

After putting up a career-high and team-record 206 tackles in 1996, Chris Spielman, Buffalo's hardworking linebacker who would often be seen wearing his game face regardless of whether there was a game that day or not, was stopped midway through the 1997 campaign. Not by a massive offensive tackle trying to clear a path, but by an injury. A serious injury! It occurred during a Monday night game in Indianapolis on October 20, while tackling Colts running back Lamont Warren.

"I was paralyzed for a few seconds, then got up. It was toward the end, so I finished the game," said Spielman. "And then the next week [versus the Broncos], it happened like three more times. I didn't really say anything immediately after the Indianapolis game. I said something after the Denver game, and that's when they discovered that my disc had exploded onto my spinal cord. That's why I was having bouts of paralysis."

Spielman's reaction? "Probably that I should get this checked out, something's not right. But when you're all caught up in the moment of the game, as a player, for me anyway, I had a feeling of invincibility. Like nothing could be wrong with me. My code was if I'm walking, I can play. So I was having these little bouts, but it would always come back, and I wouldn't have any other symptoms. Looking back on it now, I wasn't very smart. Stupid! But you know, as a player, you get yourself in a mind-set, you get whooped up, and you're going to do everything in the world to play and produce. Thankfully, I had the good sense to finally seek medical attention."

The injury required surgery to fuse two vertebrae. Eight months of rehabilitation followed, and by June 1998 he felt healthy enough to return to the game. But all the workouts, all the sweat, all the determination that he experienced while getting physically ready could not help with what he faced next.

During a self-examination, his wife, Stephanie, discovered a lump in her right breast and underwent a mastectomy after two tumors were discovered. Understandably, playing football again was no longer important. The Spielmans would face months of aggressive chemotherapy together. Chris decided to step away from the game and help take care of his wife and their two young children.

Spielman skipped training camp and was not seen around Orchard Park until he showed up unexpectedly and joined his teammates on the sideline for Buffalo's game against San Francisco on October 4. His return was acknowledged by the 76,615 fans in attendance with a standing ovation.

"I think that people respected the decision that I made," Spielman said. "It was an easy decision to make, but it still felt like you were letting people down. I certainly made the right decision, don't get me wrong. I felt like the people in Buffalo, for the two years, treated me great, and I loved playing there and being a part of it, but I still felt like I let them down. I guess it justified my decision to not play football because I got a standing ovation. It made me feel good, obviously. I guess that I was accepted as a Buffalo Bill."

sources

Carroll, Bob, Michael Gershman, David Neft, John Thorn, and the Elias Sports Bureau. *Total Football: The Official Encyclopedia of the National Football League.* New York: Harper Collins Publishers, 1999.

Maiorana, Sal. *Relentless: The Hard-Hitting History of Buffalo Bills Football.* Lenexa, KS: Quality Sports Publications, 1994.

Maiorana, Sal. *Relentless: The Hard-Hitting History of Buffalo Bills Football, Vol. II.* Coal Valley, IL: Quality Sports Publications, 2000.